Chris Sidwells is a freelance writer, editor and photographer whose words and/or photographs appear in every edition of Britain's best-selling cycling magazine, *Cycling Weekly*. His most recent project has been to produce and edit ten very successful bookazines in a series called Cycling Legends for Time Inc., which carry the *Cycling Weekly* brand. Chris also writes for *Cycle Sport* and *Cycling Active*. In addition he has carried out commissions for *Cycling Plus*, *GQ Magazine*, *Men's Fitness*, *Running Fitness*, the *Sunday Times*, the *Guardian* and the BBC.

He also works as a regular cycling pundit for several BBC local radio stations, including working on BBC Radio Sheffield's live coverage of the 2014 Tour de France Grand Depart in Yorkshire and the Tour de Yorkshire.

Chris has written, or part-written, 17 books on cycling, 3 of them coffee-table guide books, in the 12 years he has worked in this business, supplying photographs as well as words for 3 of them. His books, many of which have gone to multiple editions and been bestsellers in their genre, cover every aspect of cycling, and in total they have been translated into 24 languages.

His most recent book is a collaboration with Chris Boardman called *The Biography of the Modern Bike*, published by Octopus in 2015. He is currently writing a book on the history of cycling jerseys, and under his own publishing brand www.cyclinglegends.co.uk in 2015 he published the British pioneer professional Barry Hoban's autobiography, *Vas-y Barry*.

Chris has a degree in geology, is a qualified cycling coach and fitness instructor and is an active cyclist with years of racing and riding experience in every aspect of the sport. He has won races in every cycling discipline, road, track and off-road, and in every age group from youth to masters.

WILD CYCLING

A POCKET GUIDE TO 50 GREAT RIDES OFF THE BEATEN TRACK IN BRITAIN

CHRIS SIDWELLS

Dedication
To all wild cyclists everywhere

ROBINSON
First published in Great Britain in 2017
by Robinson

1 2 3 4 5 6 7 8 9 10

A CIP catalogue record for this book is available from the British Library.

ISBN: 978-1-47213-979-5

Typeset in Adelle Sans and Whitman
Designed by Andrew Barron @ Thextension
Maps & diagrams by Cedric Knight
Printed and bound in China

Robinson
An imprint of
Little, Brown Book Group
Carmelite House
50 Victoria Embankment
London EC4Y 0DZ

An Hachette UK Company
www.hachette.co.uk

www.littlebrown.co.uk

Contents

1

What is Wild Cycling?

It can be lots of things, from short ambles through country lanes to off-the-grid bike adventures in a far-off wilderness. For me, though, wild cycling means using bridleways, trails and tiny lanes to explore the countryside. Almost any bike, aside from the lightest thoroughbred racers, will do, although rougher trails require bikes with some specific off-road capability. So cyclo-cross, gravel or mountain bikes are the best for wild cycling, but there are off-the-beaten-track rides you can do on almost any bike, if you look for them. This book will help you find those rides.

It presents 50 off-the-beaten-track rides from all over the UK, but they are by no means prescriptive. Wild rides are not like hills: this book doesn't say, 'Here are 50 rides – go and do them, tick them off.' Instead they are suggestions; each one has further routes radiating out from it, as well as being an introduction to the wild-cycling potential of a wide range of locations in mainland UK, and to the concept of wild cycling anywhere.

I chose them because they are in places I know, places I've cycled in, and I've spread them throughout the country as best I can. In some I remember the people who showed me them, or an incident or feature connected with them. Others are done in the same spirit as the mountaineer's mantra: 'Because it's there.'

Some rides require the inclusion of short stretches of main road, for which I apologise, but they are only used where necessary to link things together and create interesting and varied routes. It was also necessary to demonstrate that there are wild rides almost anywhere, if you look. I've even included a few in the heart of a city, and in other built-up areas.

Wild cycling is a release: it's getting back to nature, and even more to our collective childhoods. That's when most of us first got bikes. Remember how it felt? The freedom, the means to roam and discover places, and the visceral rush of bombing through the woods and bouncing over the bumps. It's escaping traffic, living in the moment – but above all wild cycling is child-like fun.

But now you're older fun requires planning, and your planning documents are the series of British Ordnance Survey (OS) 1:50,000-scale Landranger maps. They are big enough to cover the sort of area a cyclist can range around, and they contain crucial information in an easy-to-assimilate form.

To plan your own wild rides you need to know the rights of way for cyclists. The main off-road rights are along bridleways, which are represented on OS Landranger maps by long-dashed red lines. Short-dashed red lines are footpaths, and at the moment, in England at least, cyclists aren't allowed to ride along footpaths.

However, even as I write, the opening-up of some footpaths to cyclists is being considered in official circles.

The rides in this book mostly use bridleways and tiny lanes, shown in yellow on Landranger maps, with the width of yellow broadly proportional to the width of the lane. Other small lanes are shown by parallel narrow black lines, although there are often local rights in force on these roads. The yellow ones are much more dependable.

You'll often find that lanes change to bridleways and back again. This is because they were often the earliest roads. You come across a good example of this on Ride 36, Kinder Trespass, where the tiny lane going east out of Hayfield changes to bridleway after Coldwell Clough, then continues up Oaken Clough, 'clough' being a north-country dialect word for valley, up past Edale Cross and down Jacob's Ladder into Edale. This used to be the main route between the Hayfield and Edale, both vital farming areas. It was a hard way, but a much shorter one than the easier routes that have become main roads, like Snake Pass. The Edale Cross route was perfect for walkers and packhorses, which was how goods used to be carried in mountainous areas. Later, when motor vehicles took over transport and travel, roads like Snake Pass came into their own, leaving routes like Edale Cross to feet, hooves and two wheels.

The history of roads is fascinating, although way beyond the remit of this book. Just be thankful that the old ways are impossible for motors – it means they are perfect for cyclists. Drovers' roads are another kind of old route you find in Great Britain. A place name or road name that ends in 'drove' indicates a drovers' road. These were used for moving livestock to and from markets. They feature in this book quite a lot.

So try as many of the 50 routes I've suggested as you like, and use them to plan others and discover more wonderful places. On some rides I've indicated places where you could bolt on extra loops, or where there are other interesting places to ride close by. I've also avoided making all the 50 rides great and gruelling adventures, because I want them to be accessible to as many people as possible.

The rides are starting-points, templates for further exploration using OS maps, or their digital version Memory Map. Memory Map is quite a thing to work with, because you get the whole of the country on your computer screen, and it's a lot of fun planning your route at home without having to unfold a lot of maps. I hope you enjoy the book and find it useful, and I wish you many years of happy wild cycling.

2

What Do You Need?

The first thing is a well-maintained bike. Bike breakdowns are a pain, and in remote places they can quickly become a problem. Rough trails demand more from a bike than riding on smooth roads – another reason to get a good maintenance programme established, and regularly replace any component as soon as it shows signs of wear. There are plenty of books for guidance on this, and any bike shop with a qualified mechanic will help, advise and provide a regular check-and-maintenance regime.

Bikes with off-road capability – cyclo-cross, gravel and mountain bikes – are best suited to wild cycling, but a road or touring bike, so long as you can fit wide robust tyres to it, is fine for some of the rides in this book. Tyres, though, are key.

I use a cyclo-cross bike for my wild rides. I find it can cope with most off-road terrain, and on the rare occasions it's not quite up to the terrain it is light enough to pick up and carry. The one modification I make is swapping knobbly off-road tyres for a more all-round tyre with plenty of puncture protection. I've used knobbly tyres, but I find they are a drag on road sections and hard-packed trail. My favourite tyres now are Schwalbe Marathon Plus, and – I know I'll jinx it by saying this – in thousands of off-road miles I've not had one puncture. That's important.

Punctures are a drag at any time, but punctures in the wild are bad news. So fit good-quality, heavy-duty tyres and check them regularly. Any cuts, bulges, scuffs or excessive wear mean you need a new tyre. It's a golden rule.

The other golden rule of wild cycling is take an Ordnance Survey map of the area where you are riding, and an old-fashioned compass. GPS devices are a great help, but maps don't run on batteries, they don't require satellite coverage, and they never let you down. The same goes for a standard compass.

With a map and a compass you always know where you are. OS maps are orientated roughly north-to-south. So lay the map out, place the compass on top of it and line the top of the map up with where the compass points north. Face that direction. The map is then roughly orientated, and you should be able to relate the features illustrated on it to features you can see. That's not exact, but it's a helpful start.

There are variations, and OS Landranger maps can be fully orientated by joining a circle on their bottom edge, south, to the point on the protractor scale at the top of the map at the angle estimated for the current year. Details of this technique are available on sites like www.maptools.com/tutorials/plotting/plotting-a-bearing. You could also enrol on a good map-reading course. It's worth signing up to one if you are unsure how to use OS maps properly.

A map and compass fit easily into standard cycling jerseys, and it is important to use specific cycling kit, not normal outdoor clothes, and dress according to the weather. Check two weather forecasts before long wild rides, and if you are going high always carry a cycling-specific rucksack. It doesn't need to be big, but it should contain a full set of water- and windproof clothing, and extra gloves in case the weather turns really bad. It can get very cold very quickly above 300 metres or 1,000 feet in Britain, even in summer. Take a first aid kit, a whistle to attract attention if you have an accident, and emergency food and drinks. You could even spoil yourself: with a rucksack you can do it in style and carry a picnic.

Then there are also things you must take with you on any ride. Two spare tubes and a set of tyre levers, plus a multi-tool, and a puncture repair kit in case you have more than two punctures. These will all fit in a small under-the-saddle bag. Take your mobile phone and some money with you as well.

And if you are going into mountain areas, once you plan your route tell somebody where you are going, and then stick to it. That goes a bit against the free-roving wild-cycling idea, but mountains should be treated with extra respect. If you see a better line or another way, return to explore it another day.

Take enough food and drinks for the level of ride you are doing. Two-litre bottles of liquid can be carried in standard bike-bottle cages. Energy bars, gels, small cakes and bananas, meanwhile, fit nicely into cycling jersey pockets. Take more than you think you'll need; same goes for liquid.

Finally, there are some riding skills that will help you stay safe and enjoy wild cycling even more. There are books on technique that you can buy, but I've listed some basic skills here that will help you.

Avoiding cracks, potholes and loose surfaces

Riding into any of the above should be avoided if possible. The key skill is focusing on where you want to go, not on what you want to avoid.

When you come to a challenging trail it is worth stopping first to plot the best, and that means smoothest and surest, line through it. Then focus on that and nothing else. And coax your bike rather than bully it along.

The smoothest line on many tracks is over to one side or the other, away from the middle. The thing is, tracks often get worn concave, so keeping to one side means riding on a camber, and gravity wants to pull your bike downwards. Counteract this by leaning slightly towards the side you want to stay on, and pushing slightly harder on the pedal furthest from the trail edge:

ORBEA
ORBEA
CNP

it helps push you back up where you need to be.

Sometimes it's necessary to cross a section of trail you'd rather avoid. Pick the smoothest way across, and head straight over it. Don't try to turn on it or brake; get your speed right before you cross it.

Be light, get out of the saddle, stay loose, keep your weight spread evenly over your bike and let the bike move up and down underneath you, flexing your arms and legs to absorb the bumps and shocks.

Riding rocky descents

Get out of the saddle before the rocky section. Hold the brake levers from above and slightly bend your elbows ready to absorb bumps. Have your cranks parallel with the ground and bend your knees slightly too.

Place your hips, which are your centre of gravity, over the saddle, or just behind it if it's steep, and only brake to adjust your speed when going in a straight line. The steeper the descent, the further back your hips should go, because descending affects brake bias, effectively putting more bias on the front brake. Pushing your hips back counteracts this.

Pick your line through the rocky bit, steering by using your weight to influence the direction of your bike by shifting your upper body one way or another. Try to keep your bike straight and let it move up and down over bumps, moving your legs and arms to absorb shocks so they don't knock you off-line.

Bunny hop

Doing a small modified hop is very useful if logs, branches or small rocks are in your path. It means you don't have to dismount and carry your bike over them.

Approach the obstacle with a bit of speed and aim to go over it where the ground on the other side looks solid. As you get closer, get out of the saddle slightly.

Just before your front wheel hits the obstacle, give a hard pull up and back on your handlebars to lift the wheel. Move your body back a bit at the same time so the front wheel is un-weighted.

Once the front wheel is over, shift your body weight forward and flick both feet upwards to lift the back wheel over the obstacle. It doesn't matter if it touches it: so long as your back wheel is un-weighted it will follow your front.

Climbing out of the saddle on loose surfaces

Most of the time the best way to climb is sitting in the saddle and using a low gear. That rule is the same on-road and off-, only it's even more important off-road because sitting in the saddle keeps weight over the rear wheel, loading it to maintain traction with the ground.

However, as with some road climbs, there are off-road slopes that are so steep you have to get out of the saddle, so that back, shoulder and arm muscles can help apply power to the pedals. On the road you do this by getting right over the bike's changed centre of gravity, so moving your whole body upwards and forwards.

But this unloads the rear wheel, and on loose surfaces you will lose traction and the rear wheel could spin, maybe causing you to stop, or in extreme cases stall and fall off your bike. To prevent this you must shift as much of your weight backwards as possible while climbing out of the saddle on loose stuff. Ride with straight arms and try to keep your bottom hovering just over the saddle.

Cornering on loose surfaces

Approach a right corner well over to your left. Look into the corner and visualise your line through it, cutting into the apex (inside the middle of the corner) and coming out on the left of the trail again. The line should avoid any potholes or puddles. Look for where the surface has been worn by tyres, because tyres form little berms that you can follow to help round the corner. Brake to reduce speed only when you are travelling in a straight line, and shift to a lower gear before you enter the corner to help you accelerate out of the other side.

Keep your inside knee up, press down on your outside pedal and lean your bike into the corner, aiming for the line through the apex you've chosen. If you feel your wheels slip, press harder on the outside leg and move your upper body to the outside as well. Do not brake during the corner, because doing so will make the bike track straight, which means you might not get round the corner. It also destabilizes your bike.

Continue freewheeling through the corner, aiming to end up on the left edge of the trail once it's going straight again. Start pedalling when you are travelling in a straight line.

Hopping a pothole

Potholes should always be avoided. The best you might get from hitting a big one is an impact puncture. A broken wheel is another possibility; so is a trip over the handlebars and an undignified crash. However, potholes aren't always easy to see, and this is a 'get-out-of-jail' skill if you simply cannot avoid hitting a pothole. Basically, you jump your bike over it.

As soon as you see the pothole, get out of the saddle and have your cranks parallel to the floor. Then, just before your front wheel would hit the hole, pull up and back on your handlebars and move your body weight back. Just a split second after you lift the front wheel, close your knees and pull up on the pedals with your feet. This should hop the back wheel over the pothole, but even if the back wheel clips it, this action unloads it, so you should come through unscathed.

Riding through soft sand

It's impossible to steer through soft sand; you have to let the bike go where it wants. However, there are two factors that help you stay in control: pick the best line through the loose sand, and provide lots of power to blast your bike through. The best line is the one that requires the least change of direction, so locate where you want to go, and aim for that. A couple of subtleties are that the firmest line often has the most tyre tracks through it, or it can be indicated by the presence of standing water. Look for these clues.

Don't approach too fast, or the change of surface can take your front wheel from under you, but once in the sand apply maximum power. Pedal seated to give your rear wheel good traction. Hold the handlebars firmly, but relax your shoulders and arms.

Give an extra-hard kick as soon as your front wheel makes contact with a harder surface, then you can pedal easy for a bit to recover. If there is lots of loose sand on a ride it's best to carry your bike over it, because sand wears out bike equipment like nothing else. Always clean your bike after a sandy ride.

Dismount and carry your bike

Hold the tops of your brake levers so you can control your speed. Brake until you are going slowly enough to jump off and unclip your right foot. It's possible with practice to dismount while moving, but it's best at first to come almost to a halt, then unclip your left foot and jump off.

With your left hand still holding the top of the handlebars, grab the bike's top tube with your right hand and lift it up towards your right shoulder.

Feed the bike onto your shoulder with your right hand, and remove the left from the handlebars. Once the bike sits on your shoulder with its weight evenly distributed, bring your right arm around the front of it and get hold of the handlebars to steady the bike. Start walking.

3

The South and East

1 Chalk Cliffs and Curious Sound Mirrors

East Kent coastal ride along the coast to Dover with memories of war ever-present

DIFFICULTY RATING **6/10** WILDNESS RATING **5/10**

There are so many interesting distractions on this lovely loop around the east Kent coast that it's worth adding at least an hour for stops at various places to take it all in. As well as the views across the English Channel, with craft of all shapes and sizes plying their trade or pleasure, there's the Battle of Britain memorial and its recently opened visitor centre. A couple of miles further east there's a concrete sound mirror, arresting and mysterious as it looks out to sea from Abbot's Cliff – but more of that later.

Apart from a short stretch of country lane at the end, the whole route follows waymarked routes from the National Cycle Network (NCN), which makes light work of map reading and, in a relatively busy part of east Kent, ensures that traffic is either light or banished altogether.

We begin the ride in Folkestone, a revived and sizeable town that services the adjacent Channel Tunnel terminal and, thanks to the new high-speed railway line, is less than an hour from London. Folkestone is a few minutes off junction 13 of the M20. Heading east along the A259, direction 'Harbour', will bring you down to the old quayside on the east side of the town. There's lots of parking, but you will have to pay. Have a pre-ride coffee or post-ride fish and chips in the harbour-side Captain's Table café – both are good, but don't forget: the café is cash only.

Now for the bad news: from the cobbled alleyways of the harbour there's a big climb out of Folkestone through residential streets, following NCN route 2, also known as the Chalk and Channel Way. Take your time and keep the gears low; it's steep in places, but the difficulty is it goes on and on out of town.

At one point you have to dismount to cross the old Dover road, and then it

FACT FILE

Where Folkestone on the Kent coast

OS grid ref TR 2339 3626

Start/Finish Folkestone harbour

Ride distance 28.4 kilometres (17.75 miles)

Highest points Capel-le-Ferne (169 metres), Dover Hill (168 metres)

Approximate time 2 hours

CHALK CLIFFS AND CURIOUS SOUND MIRRORS

Track Elevation

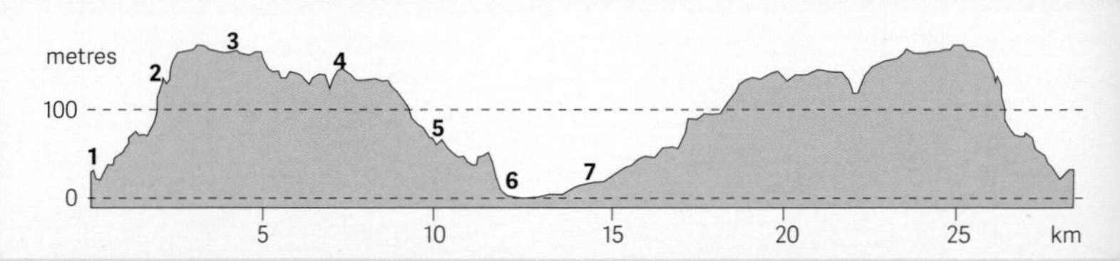

1 Start/Finish
2 Steep uphill
3 Battle of Britain Memorial
4 Trail section, muddy in places
5 The Sound Mirror
6 Follow NCN route 2 signs through Dover
7 Pick NCN route 17 sign here

gets interesting, as you leave the urban traffic and pick up the cycleway and minor road that lead to the summit. When you get there there's a pavement bike path heading east; follow it and you soon reach the entrance to the Battle of Britain memorial. It's fascinating as well as heroic.

The memorial commemorates the pilots who in 1940 saved Britain from invasion by the Nazis. There's a moving statue of a solitary airman seated on the ground in the middle of a big grass circle, looking out to sea. There are also scale models of a Spitfire and a Hurricane, and a new visitor centre with bike parking.

A right fork after the memorial picks up a minor road through Capel-le-Ferne, where an assortment of weather-beaten houses and bungalows sit not far from the cliff tops. No need to rush on this gentle descent as, whatever the weather, views over the Channel never fail to stir the soul of an islander. There's a fun café along here: the Cliff Top Café, nestled in the cliffs. It's well worth a stop to take in the view with a comforting cuppa.

In the distance there's Dover with its rambling castle, the biggest in England, substantially fortified by William the Conqueror, and a vital communications centre and hospital during the Second World War. It's also where a Tour de France stage started in 1994, during the second-ever visit of the world's biggest bike race to the UK.

Stay on the narrow pavement for the short stretch on the B2011. It's only a few hundred metres before the NCN swings off on a metalled driveway back up towards the cliffs. When I came through, at least one NCN sign was a bit knocked-about, so best to have the local map (OS179) to hand. At the top of this short climb the road becomes a stony track, and stays that way as it wends its way into Dover. In places it's little more than a muddy path, so take it easy and pick the right lines around the puddles and gloop.

On Abbot's Cliff, halfway between Folkestone and Dover, stands the imposing concrete sound mirror. It looks like something from the Second World War, or even a 1950s sci-fi movie, but it is a relic of the First World War. Several sound mirrors were built back then around the south and north-east coasts of Britain. They were an attempt at early detection of

Bianchi

air raids, and they worked on slower planes, but as speeds increased they were less useful, then totally surpassed by radar. Very few remain today.

There are many reasons to stop throughout this ride. No sooner are you back in the saddle than what looks like an open book is lying in the grass on the next stony climb. It's one of several small concrete and bronze plaques celebrating the unique flora and fauna of the area.

With the roar of trucks heading for the Port of Dover growing ever more apparent, the NCN route drops down beside the M20 before crossing a footbridge and into the back streets of Dover. The waymarked NCN route east guides you down to the seafront, but keep a keen lookout for the signs. It then continues east out of Dover to link up with NCN route 17, the Coast-to-Cathedral route, which really means Dover to Canterbury, the start of this ride's return leg to Folkestone via West Hougham.

There's a climb out of Dover, and the section after it is on minor roads open to traffic. They are quiet lanes, though, often with gravel and mud down the centre of them, which get a bit churned up in winter. Follow NCN route 17 around the village of West Hougham, and take either of the next two left turns in Hockley Sole to return to Capel-le-Ferne, where you start the speedy descent to Folkestone on NCN route 2.

2 White Roads and South Downs
The South Downs from above and below

DIFFICULTY RATING **6/10** WILDNESS RATING **6/10**

This is a splendid ride to experience cycling along the beautiful chalk uplands of the South Downs, but there are many more. The whole area is criss-crossed by bridleways, back roads and bike-accessible trails. Some of the lower ones look similar to the white roads of Tuscany, the Strade Bianchi, made famous in cycling by a race of the same name. The higher trails have a unique South Downs character.

You will see the Downs in all their shapely glory from the low trails, then climb onto their green, rounded summits, where there are stunning views of sea and countryside. There are also plenty of side trails to explore along the way.

Alfriston is a good place to start, because of its historic buildings and the charming Cuckmere River. There are also two car parks on the higher section of this ride, which I'll mention when we get there, and they would make good starts and finishes as well.

One thing, though, whether you start in Alfriston or go through it mid-ride: check out the winged wheel symbol outside Ye Olde Smugglers Inne on Waterloo Square – it's right outside the door. Winged wheels were an early rating system devised by the Cyclists' Touring Club (CTC), now rebranded as Cycling UK. Established in 1881, they were awarded to eating places and hotels CTC officials had inspected and arranged special rates with for their club members.

Head north from the Smugglers to a crossroads where the metalled road goes sharp right, and carry on straight to pick up a trail. This takes you along the undulating base of the South Downs, through a glorious patchwork of arable fields.

Continue on the trail to Bo-Peep

FACT FILE

Where The eastern end of the South Downs, quite close to where they end at Beachy Head

OS grid ref TQ 5188 0311

Start/Finish Afriston

Ride distance 16 kilometres (10 miles)

Highest point Firle Beacon (217 metres)

Approximate time 2 hours

WHITE ROADS AND SOUTH DOWNS

Track Elevation

1 Start
2 Using this road cuts the ride in half
3 Take the left trail fork
4 Rutted surface
5 Steep up hill
6 Highest point of the ride

Farm, where you cross a metalled road, and carry straight to a fork in the trail at a copse. Take the left fork, then go straight at the next trail junction, and around some farm buildings near Firle Place, a 15th-century manor built with Caen stone in French Chateau style. It's the family seat of the Gage family. The current resident, Nicholas Gage, is the eighth Viscount Gage; his ancestors include John Gage, a close adviser to King Henry VIII.

The trail surface is quite good on the early part of this ride, but after Bo-Peep Farm it becomes rough, with long ruts where excess water appears to run along the trail. Take care on this section and avoid the ruts. Eventually you reach a lane called Firle Bostal; turn left, then climb the steep hill, which at 1.8 kilometres long, with an average gradient of 7.5%, is a toughie.

Eventually, as the gradient begins to relent, you reach a car park on your left. Enter that and look for a distinct, well-worn trail going off to your left. That's the South Downs Way, and you follow it along the spine of the Downs all the way back into Alfriston.

The surface is good for this section, mostly tractor tracks with a soft grassy middle, but watch out for dreamy sheep stepping out in front of you; they rule up here. Look out too for where some of the tractor tracks are deep. It's better to avoid them by riding the grassy bits in between.

After about a mile of steady climbing you reach the top of Firle Beacon, the high point of this ride, where a stop is recommended to take in the 360-degree view. East and west are the rolling green hills of the South Downs. The sea, Newhaven and the English Channel lie to the south. Pevensey Levels shimmer in the north-east, while the landscape of the Low and High Weald spreads all the way to the northern horizon. Weald is an old English word for forest, and the land is dotted with seductive woods – public ones waiting to be explored, and smaller, more private enclosures.

Pressing on east from the summit of Firle Beacon there's a gentle descent for 500 metres, before a short stiff climb to the top of Bostal Hill. The low circular mounds here are part of a Bronze Age burial ground, the last mound lying on a small shelf just east of the summit of Bostal Hill. It precedes the final downward rush into Alfriston, to the second of the car park start/finish options.

While in the town try to visit Dene car park between West Street and North Street, to see the Alfriston Lock-Up. It's believed to be a holding cell used by early law officers, mostly for holding drunks before letting them go next day. I wonder how many happy and not so happy drunks spent a night clamped up inside this tiny flint building?

3 Surrey Hills Leg-Slapper

In Surrey's 'little Switzerland' there are enough tracks and paths to lose yourself for hours

DIFFICULTY RATING **6/10** WILDNESS RATING **5/10**

No wonder this area of Surrey, not much more than 30 miles from central London, has been and still is a much-loved playground for all kinds of cyclists. It's sometimes called Little Switzerland because of its hills, but it's a tree-covered Little Switzerland with a labyrinth of narrow lanes and endless off-road tracks and bridleways. And they are just waiting to be explored.

Start at the village green at Holmbury St Mary, in the shadow of St Mary's church, which looks a bit Swiss. The Royal Oak pub there offered their car park on the promise of buying a drink there after the ride, which was kept, naturally.

FACT FILE

Where Holmbury St Mary is 8 kilometres south-west of Dorking, which is on the A24 8 kilometres south of junction 9 of the M25

OS grid ref TQ 1099 4455

Start/Finish Holmbury St Mary

Ride distance 16.5 kilometres (10.3 miles)

Highest point Leith Hill (294 metres)

Approximate time 2 hours

Most of this ride is off-road, so a conventional road or touring bike isn't suitable. A cyclo-cross or gravel bike, or better still a mountain bike, are the bikes to use for Surrey tracks and trails, which in winter are quite muddy in places. The little lanes, although a joy, tend to carry some pretty hefty potholes too.

This ride is also quite rocky in places, requiring some technical skills, and there are the off-road rider's nemesis, slippery tree roots, to contend with. Wherever possible try to cross tree roots at right angles; you can always walk some of the trickier sections, as I did. It makes this ride no less enjoyable.

Just outside Holmbury St Mary, then, going south past the church on the B2126 Horsham Road, you turn left into Pasture Wood Road and almost immediately pick up the fingerpost on the right for the Greensand Way, which is followed for a fair chunk of the ride. The Greensand Way is a 108-mile footpath that follows the Greensand Ridge along the east–west axis of the Surrey Hills. Greensand is a sandstone laid

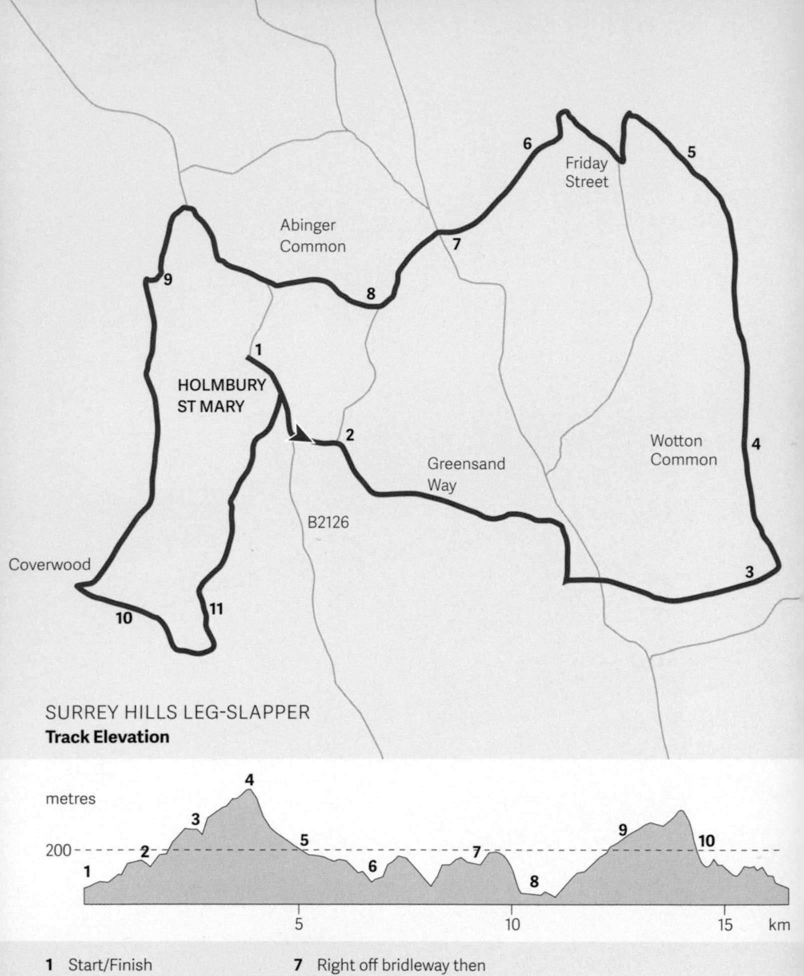

1 Start/Finish
2 Right onto Greensand Way
3 Leith Hill
4 Long descent
5 Take left fork
6 Follow bridleway on left
7 Right off bridleway then cross the road
8 Bridleway
9 Road becomes bridleway
10 Sand Hill climb
11 Road back to Holmbury

down during the Lower Cretaceous period, so 100 to 145 million years ago, which gets its name from silty or clay material mixed with sand.

Off-road from here, it's single-track heaven through lovely mixed woodland, with glimpses of the surrounding hills as you climb gently towards the second-highest point in south-east England, Leith Hill. The highest is Walbury Hill, near Hungerford in West Berkshire, but there's only three metres in it. Leith Hill is 294 metres to Walbury's 297, but Leith Hill has its tower.

It was built between 1755 and 1756 on the instructions of Richard Hull, then owner of Leith Hill Place, to raise the height of the hill to over 1,000 feet. It did just that, topping out at 313.5 metres (1,028 feet 6 inches). Hull himself is buried beneath the tower. The views north towards London, and on very clear days south as far as the English Channel, are fabulous. Leith Hill Tower is owned by the National Trust now, and is open to the public from 10 a.m. until 3 p.m. on weekdays, and 9 a.m. to 5 p.m. at weekends.

Next up is a long descent on the Greensand Way through the woods, which is really enjoyable. Fork left soon after the trail becomes metalled road, then turn left, and there's a short, steep road climb to Friday Street, where you go right and follow another tiny lane round to a marked bridleway section. This goes uphill and south-

west from the road junction. There are a few steps up to it, but then it's quite easy to follow through the woods to another road.

Turn right on the road you come out on, then go straight across a crossroads and follow a lane to Parkhurst, where a bridleway goes right. Join that and keep right where it forks. This leads to Felbury House. Go right on the B2126, and after one kilometre hang a left onto a lane that quickly becomes bridleway.

This is the start of a long uphill section through woodland, followed by a descent towards Coverwood car park. Just before you get to the car park turn left onto another bridleway, to begin a hard-packed sandy climb to the top of Holmbury Hill. It's a long upwards pull, but you can remain seated the whole way up and will be rewarded with fine views from the top, which was once an Iron Age fort. Continue down the steep off-road descent to a tiny lane. Go left and follow the lane along the edge of the woods all the way back to Holmbury St Mary.

4 Going Wild Inside the M25

London has quite a few wild spaces to explore by bike; get out the map and find something like this

DIFFICULTY RATING **5/10** WILDNESS RATING **4/10**

How many wild-cycling expeditions start at a motorway service station, like this one does at Clacket Lane services on the M25? Well, there are no more in this book, but if you are looking for wild spaces inside London's orbital motorway you must be creative. And Clacket Lane does have a nice rural sound. In fact, although the services are busy, they are surrounded by very nice, and in places spectacular, countryside.

Whichever side you come off the motorway, north or south, park up in a quiet corner of the services car park; Clacket Lane – yes, there is one – runs north-south just to the east of both car parks. Barriered service roads link to Clacket Lane on either side, but there's room to walk around the barriers. Get the bike out, get past the barriers and you are off into our green and pleasant land.

Whichever side of the motorway you start from, turn left out of the service road and head north. I parked on the south side, so it was a wonderful feeling leaving the soulless services, crossing the motorway bridge with the traffic thundering underneath, and setting off up a tranquil lane just yards from the old Pilgrims' Way.

Turn left onto Pilgrims' Lane, part of the ancient route from Winchester to Canterbury that meanders along the bottom of the North Downs, and there's soon mud under your tyres as you pass Pilgrims' Farm. Next up is the hamlet of Titsey: shift into your lowest gear and get ready.

Turn right and you begin to climb Titsey Hill, but you quickly go right again and you're confronted with the infamous White Lane, scene since 1955 of the Bec Cycling Club's annual hill-climb race. White Lane climbs 79 metres in less than half a mile, and

FACT FILE

Where Inside the southern section of the M25

OS grid ref TQ 4072 5720

Start/Finish Clacket Lane Services

Ride distance 25.7 kilometres (16 miles)

Highest point Top of Beddlestead Lane (263 metres)

Approximate time 2 hours

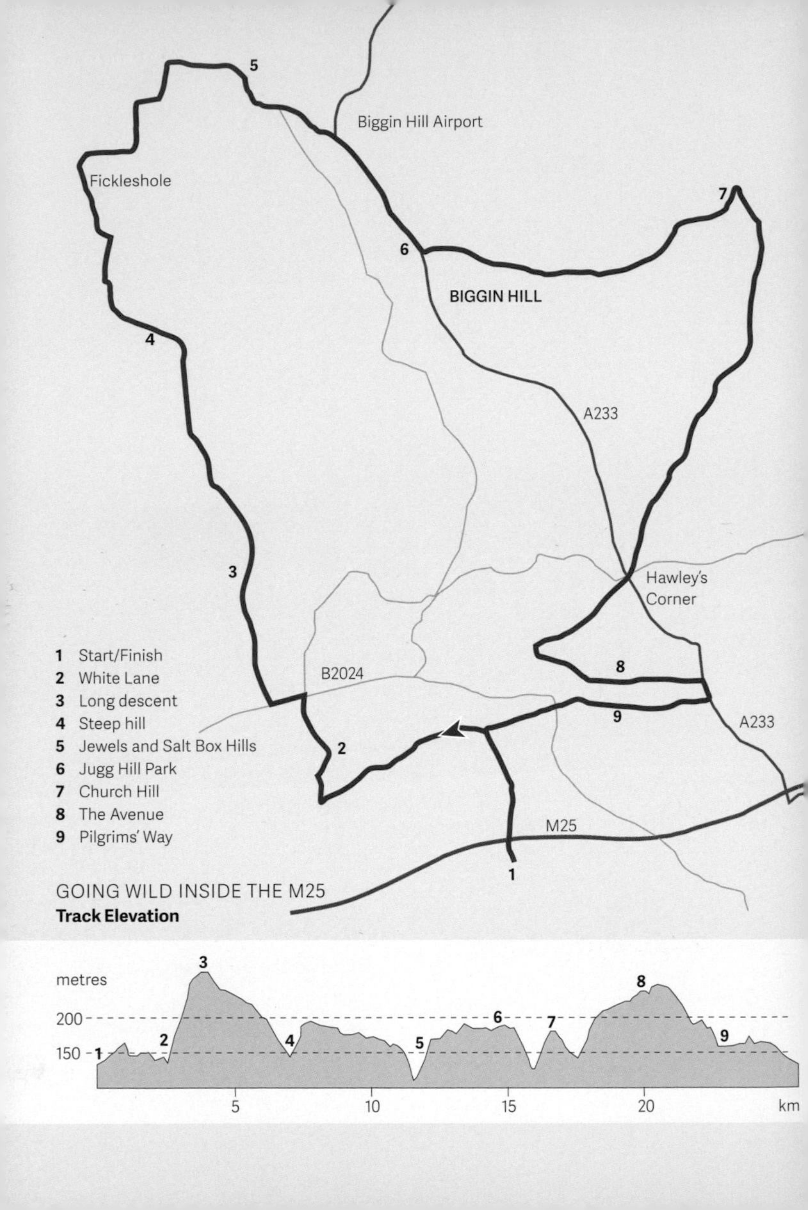
5
Biggin Hill Airport
Fickleshole
7
6
BIGGIN HILL
4
A233
3
Hawley's
Corner
1 Start/Finish
2 White Lane
3 Long descent
4 Steep hill
5 Jewels and Salt Box Hills
6 Jugg Hill Park
7 Church Hill
8 The Avenue
9 Pilgrims' Way
B2024
8
9
A233
2
M25
1
GOING WILD INSIDE THE M25
Track Elevation
metres
200
150
km
5
10
15
20

it gets steeper the higher up you go until at the top the gradient is 25%.

Don't panic about the constant humming in your ears while you climb: it's the M25, never far away on this ride, not a heart attack. Turn left at the top of the hill and ride along the busier B2024, then go first right on Beddlestead Lane, a favourite with local cyclists escaping from Croydon.

A long and in places steep descent down Beddlestead Lane is followed by a shorter, steep ascent. Continue over the crossroads to Fickleshole. Turn right there, then go right again on Sheepbarn Lane, down the steep Jewels Hill, then up the equally steep Salt Box Hill to Biggin Hill Airport. This was one of the principal fighter bases protecting London during the Second World War.

Next up is an unavoidable bit of main road. Turn right onto the A233 and head south. After about 800 metres you'll see the trees of Jugg Hill Park on your right. Start looking left for the entrance to Jail Lane, and when you see it turn left. The lane is flat at first, then goes down Berry's Hill and up Church Hill. Turn right at the top onto Cudham Lane South and head towards Cudham.

Go right on entering Cudham onto New Barn Lane. You're in real stockbroker belt here, a swish address judging by the big houses and private swimming pools. New Barn becomes Buckhurst Lane, then you reach Hawley's Corner. You are right on top

Don't panic about the constant humming in your ears while you climb: it's the M25, never far away on this ride, not a heart attack.

of the North Downs now, nearly 240 metres high.

Cross the A233 and enter Tatsfield Avenue, but quickly go left into Chestnut Avenue. The views south from here are fabulous. Follow Chestnut Avenue around to The Avenue, which descends diagonally through a wood across the slope of Betsom's Hill. Both Avenues are muddy and have loose surfaces in places. Turn right on the A233 for the last time, then almost immediate right onto the Pilgrims' Way. Cross the B2024, and turn left onto Clacket Lane and back to the services.

There are lots of places inside the M25 where you could string together wild rides like this – not just parks like Richmond, but true countryside. There are bridleways further east of here around Sidcup and Swanley. Epping Forest has lots of wild-cycling potential. And the Grand Union Canal, picked up around Abbots Langley near Watford, will take you, with good map-reading skills, to the heart of London in Paddington. Parts of the Thames Path, Esher and Epsom, and bridleways and lanes around Caterham offer further wild-cycling potential.

5 Flying with Kites
Exploring the woods and valleys of the Chiltern Hills

DIFFICULTY RATING **8/10** WILDNESS RATING **7/10**

The Chiltern Hills were inviting even before red kites returned to the skies above them, but now this majestic bird of prey only adds to the beauty and interest. The Chilterns themselves are a chalk escarpment rising steeply in the west above the Vale of Aylesbury, then dipping gently eastwards to the satellite towns around London. This is an area of wooded hills, hidden valleys and quiet spaces. It's also a great place for cycling, and this ride is a good introduction, because it opens with a section along the foot of the Chilterns.

FACT FILE

Where Chinnor is in South Oxfordshire, about 5 kilometres north-east of junction 6 of the M40

OS grid ref SP 7602 0027

Start/Finish The Ridgeway National Trail at Chinnor

Ride distance 32.5 kilometres (20.3 miles)

Highest points Christmas Common (240 metres), Ibstone Road (226 metres), Chinnor Hill (247 metres)

Approximate time 3–4 hours

So you can stand back, so to speak, and appreciate their shape before exploring their lovely folds and woods.

Red kites were persecuted from the 16th to the 19th century, in the mistaken belief that they killed livestock. In fact, red kites feed on carrion, but will kill small birds and mammals. Eventually only a handful remained in Wales, but between 1989 and 1994 they were reintroduced to the Chilterns, where they thrived. Their russet body, red, black and white wings and forked tails are a common and majestic sight in these hills today.

I started on the Ridgeway National Trail where it intersects Hill Road, just south-east of Chinnor. There are lots of other places where you could start and finish this ride, but starting here and going anti-clockwise offers a panoramic view of the western edge of the Chilterns, while enjoying a traffic-free, gently undulating first 8 kilometres.

Head south-west along the Ridgeway, across the A40 and under the M40. After 8 kilometres of undulating trail you go left on Station

Road. This climbs gently uphill at first, then becomes steeper as it climbs to the Pryton Cat Hotel, five-star accommodation for cats. The metalled road ends here, but you carry straight on up a bridleway, which is so steep you might have to dismount and push. Turn right where the bridleway meets the next road.

This is an area of wooded hills, hidden valleys and quiet spaces. It's also a great place for cycling, and this ride is a good introduction …

Follow this road through Christmas Common, keeping left onto Hollandridge Lane, then descending to a village called North End. This part of the Chilterns was famous for furniture production, done on a cottage industry basis. Individual wood turners produced legs, spindles or other parts from the beech wood they gathered, then sent them to manufacturers in Chesham and High Wycombe for assembly. Today Wycombe Wanderers football team are known as 'the Chairboys'.

In North End go straight on Holloway Lane where the main road bends right, and immediately on your left there's a bridleway. Keep right

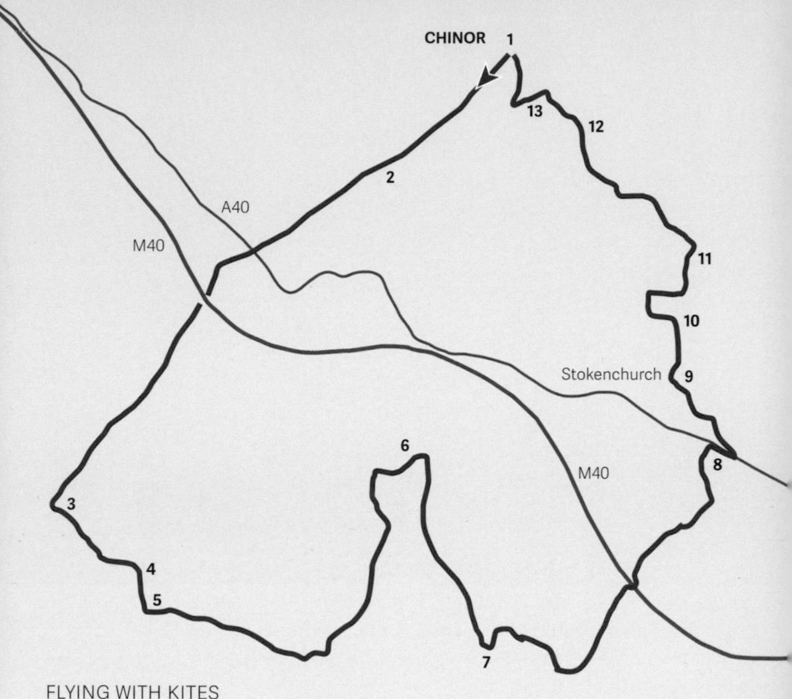

FLYING WITH KITES
Track Elevation

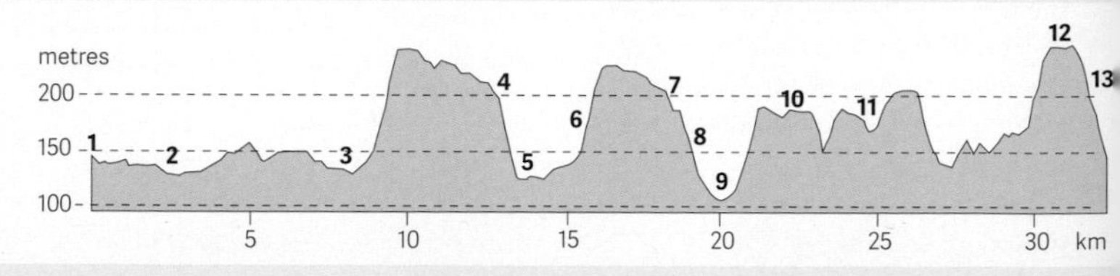

1. Start/Finish
2. Ridgeway Trail
3. Left on Station Road
4. Right on road after steep bridleway
5. Keep left through Christmas Common
6. Right on Ibstone Road
7. Left on trail at Ibstone Infants
8. Right then first left
9. Right at Waterend T-junction
10. Bridleway on left
11. Go straight on the bridleway where road bends left
12. Chinnor Road becomes Red Lane
13. Very steep road descent

where a private driveway goes off left, then continue under tree cover until you emerge at the edge of a field. Follow the bridleway north, then continue north-east across a private drive to where another bridleway joins from the south-east.

Keep on the north-east bridleway where the two join, and follow it as it bends eastwards around the Wormsley Estate. After 2.7 kilometres the bridleway runs along the western edge of Bowley's Wood. Go right at the end of this wood section and follow the bridleway east along the northern edge of the wood. The bridleway then cuts diagonally through the wood, uphill and out at Ibstone Road, where you turn right.

At Ibstone Infants School, almost at the end of the village, go left on a trail. Continue past the abandoned works and go right on a bridleway along the edge of a wood. The bridleway goes left through some trees, then along the wood's southern edge until it joins another bridleway. Go left, then right, then take the next bridleway left and follow it to Chequers Lane, where you go left.

Turn right at the junction with the B482, then go left over the M40. This is the south-eastern end of the Stokenchurch Gap, a major cutting excavated for the M40 to go through the Chilterns. Continue to the A40, where you go right, then first left on Waterend Road. Continue uphill to the

T-junction at Waterend and go right. There's a bridleway on the left where this road bends sharp right. Follow it up through a wood, which is another steep section, then along the edge of a field to Grange Farm Road. Turn right.

Take the first left up Horseshoe Road to Radnage, where you go left up Town End Road and continue straight onto a bridleway where the road bends left. This is a very distinct trail that bends left, then right, then left. Then it goes right and into Sunley Wood, another steep incline, and emerges where Chinnor Road becomes Red Lane.

Follow Red Lane left down Chinnor Hill, where another road goes right. This is a steep descent. Go sharp right at the next junction, and descend Chinnor Hill to its junction with the Ridgeway, where the ride started.

6 Dengie Marshes, Essex

A mostly on-road ride around a water-dominated landscape of big skies and lonely horizons

DIFFICULTY RATING **3/10** WILDNESS RATING **4/10**

As I said at the beginning, the 50 rides in this book aren't prescriptive: they are introductions to wild-cycling possibilities in the UK, and a starting-point for experiencing off-the-beaten-track routes. This ride in the eastern marshes of Essex is a perfect example, because it's surrounded by other interesting places to explore.

For example, the Rochford district south of the River Crouch has a lovely wild feel, and nothing could be wilder than riding on the Ministry of Defence-owned Foulness Island – although you will have to do that in company, as it's only really possible once a year as part of the Foulness Island Bike Ride. See www.thorpebayrotaryevents.co.uk for details.

North of the River Blackwater, Mersea Island is more accessible. You get onto it via an ancient man-made causeway called the Strood, which is covered at high tide and has oak piles in its construction dating from Saxon times. The network of creeks circling Mersea offers another wild-cycling opportunity.

But back to Dengie Marshes, and the start of this ride in Southminster. This is an easy one, mostly on-road, but the roads are nothing more than quiet lanes. Cycling along them, without thinking too much about navigation or surface hazards, frees up head-space to enjoy the unique landscape of the Dengie Peninsula, which is top-and-tailed by the Rivers Blackwater and Crouch and bordered by the North Sea.

Much of Dengie Marshes is inaccessible, because it is a fragile ecosystem supporting a rich and varied bird life. Most of it is a National Nature Reserve and specially protected. Even though access is restricted, quite rightly for

FACT FILE

Where The Dengie peninsula, about 16 kilometres south-east of Chelmsford

OS grid ref TQ 9583 9975

Start/Finish Southminster

Ride distance 34 kilometres (54.4 miles)

Highest point St Lawrence (34.5 metres)

Approximate time 2–3 hours

conservation, you still see plenty on this ride. Look out for hen harriers in summer; the male's striking blue-grey plumage gave rise to its nickname, the Grey Ghost.

Follow the B1201 north to Asheldham and take the first right, Hall Road. This becomes Keelings Road: follow it for a kilometre after the left turn to Dengie village. For a longer ride you could turn right down Bridgewick Lane and ride to the end of the road and back – this road runs right into the heart of Dengie Marshes, so gives a better feel of the place. Otherwise continue left on Bridgewick Lane to Tillingham.

Turn right on the B1021 and follow it to Maldon Road, where you go right to Bradwell-on-Sea. Turn right on East End Road, which is long, almost straight and probably Roman. It certainly leads straight to the Roman fort of Othona. Strictly speaking, the last 400 metres from the car park to the fort is a footpath, but you could scoot your bike along it if nobody is looking. I'll leave the choice to you.

Othona was one of nine coastal forts constructed during the third century as protection against Saxon raiders. Originally its defences were massive; its walls, arranged in trapezoid fashion, were 20 feet high and 14 feet deep,

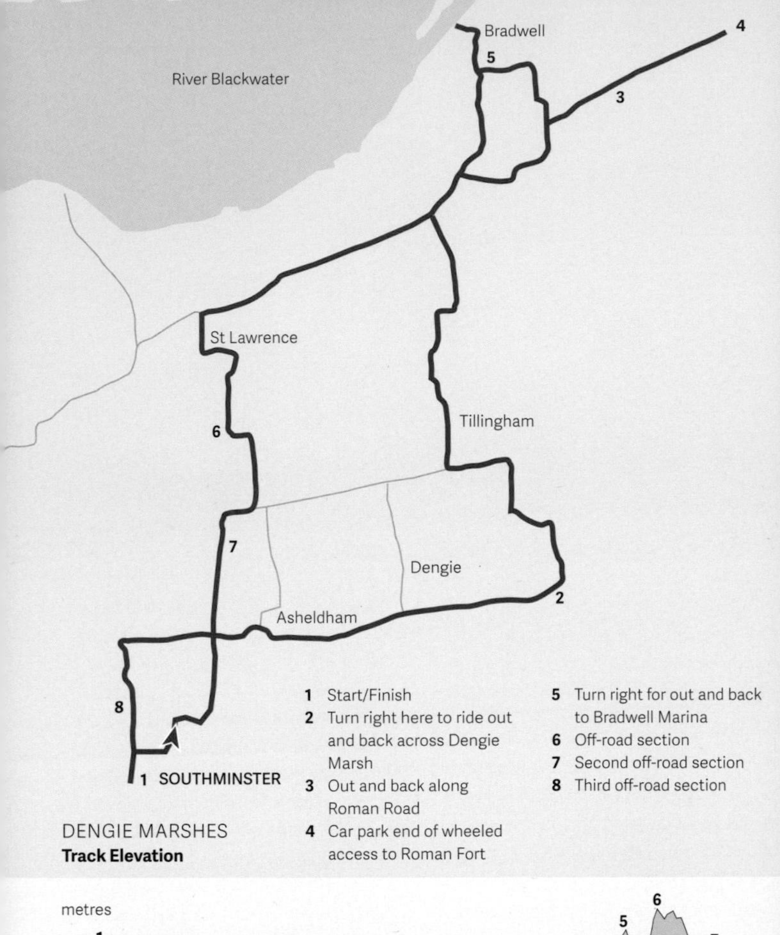

DENGIE MARSHES
Track Elevation

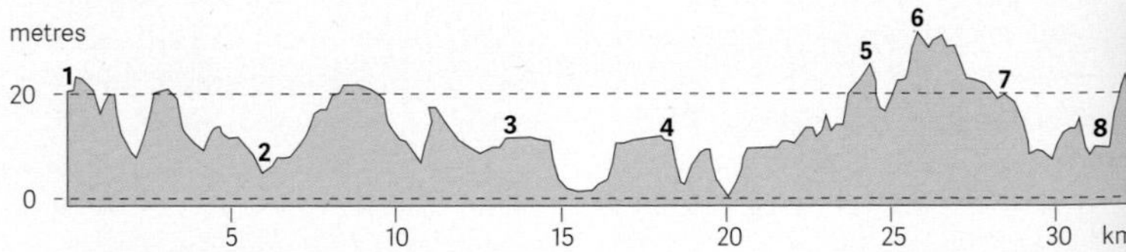

Look out for hen harriers in summer; the male's striking blue-grey plumage gave rise to its nickname, the Grey Ghost.

with towers at each corner. There were lots of Roman buildings inland from the fort, and Colchester, just to the north, was called Camulodunum, the capital of Roman Britain, Britannia, before it was destroyed during Boudicca's rebellion in AD61.

From the fort, retrace your route to Bradwell-on-Sea, turn right on High Street, then second left on Trusses Road, and right on the B1021 to visit Bradwell Marina on the River Blackwater. This is a typical Essex creek landscape, except for the backdrop of Bradwell nuclear power station. This was powered by a Magnox reactor, but has now been decommissioned. There are plans to build a new nuclear plant here.

Retrace your route south on the B1021, and go first right on Maldon Road, which runs parallel to the River Blackwater. Turn left to St Lawrence, go left again at the T-junction, but at the 90-degree left-hand bend look for a bridleway on your right. This is the first of three off-road sections.

Go right on the bridleway, which bends sharply left, then goes south along the east side of the hedgerows. There's a sharp left and right after 800 metres, then the trail crosses an open field going south. Go left when it joins the drive to a private house. The trail soon switches south again, and eventually you hit Southminster Road at High House Farm.

Turn right, and look for the bridleway on your left after Rushes Lane. This trail runs south like the previous one, but west of the hedgerow; then it goes parallel with Asheldam Brook for 750 metres to Foxhall Road. Now turn right.

The final bridleway section starts on your left after a kilometre. Follow it south through Shepcotes Farm, where it becomes Shepcotes Lane. Continue into Southminster, go left on North End and right onto the B1201, and back to wherever you started from in the town.

7 Breckland Brakes

An accessible ride in an unusual landscape with a very distinctive ecosystem

DIFFICULTY RATING **5/10** WILDNESS RATING **6/10**

Breckland, also called the Brecks, is 393 square miles of sandy heathland, often forested, straddling the counties of Norfolk and Suffolk. It's bounded by the Fens to the west and the Broads to the east. Breckland is one of the driest places in the UK, and there are few hills, which makes it a perfect place for leisurely cycling.

Much of this ride follows tracks called droves, which are old drovers' roads used many years ago for moving livestock on foot. Don't be misled by the forest symbols if you are map reading: forests here are cut down regularly, so what might be standing trees on a map could be open land by the time you come to ride through. Some trees here are planted in a method unique to Breckland called Breckland Pine Rows, where tall trees stand between open fields to prevent excessive soil erosion by the wind.

There are car parks all round this ride, but I chose to start from Brandon, a nice Suffolk town of 9,500 residents. Its name means 'hill where broom grows', and broom and gorse are part of the natural flora here. They take over whenever any forest is cleared, but the forests aren't dark and intimidating like some planted pine forests. Scots pine is one of the most common trees hereabouts, because it thrives in dry conditions, and unlike some other pines it grows tall and open.

So saddle up, and head south out of Brandon on the A1065. Turn right on Church Road, which becomes Manor Road. Then turn left on Cross Street, then right on Bond Lane, which becomes The Drove, the first off-road section.

Follow this track until Lakenheath Station, keeping your eyes peeled for

FACT FILE

Where Brandon is 8 kilometres north-west of Thetford, and 40 kilometres north-east of Cambridge

OS grid ref TL 7838 8660

Start/Finish Brandon town centre

Ride distance 33 kilometres (20.65 miles)

Highest point East end of Harling Drove (34 metres)

Approximate time 2–3 hours

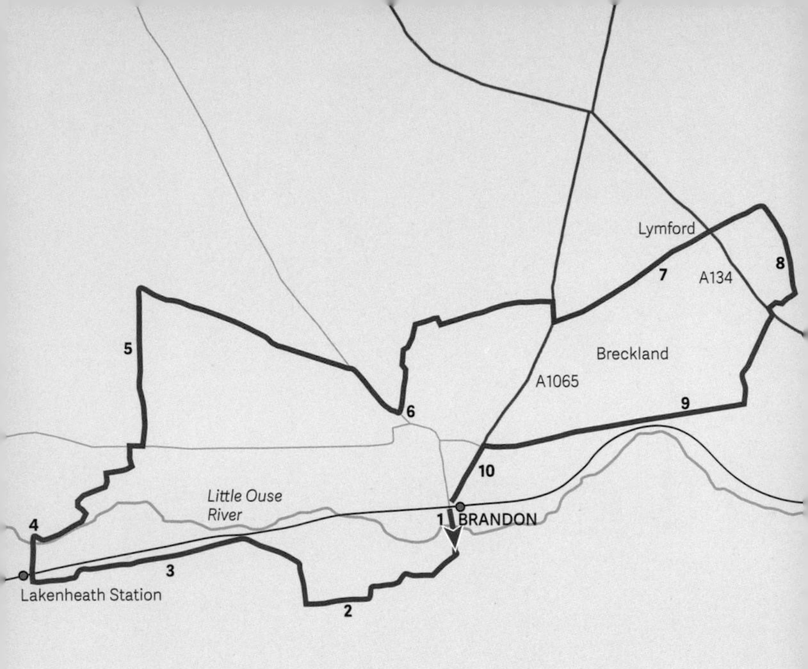

BRECKLAND BRAKES
Track Elevation

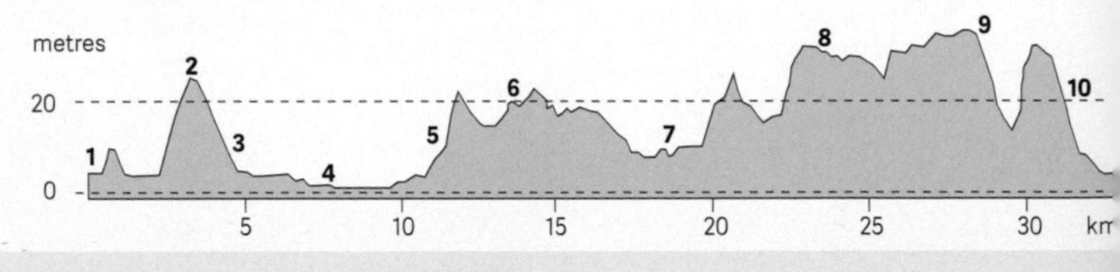

1 Start/Finish
2 Bond Lane which becomes The Drove
3 Long off-road section
4 Go past bridge, look for entrance on right to join up with Ouse embankment
5 Mill Drift
6 All Saints
7 Road section
8 Off-road
9 Harling Drove
10 Busy A-road

Breckland is one of the driest places in the UK, and there are few hills, which makes it a perfect place for leisurely cycling.

F-15 Strike Eagles taking off from the American air base at RAF Lakenheath to the south. Turn right when you get to a road, ride across the bridge over the Little Ouse, and then look for a track on your right. Go left along the river bank, then left again over the sluices. Then turn right on Nursery Lane.

Turn right in Hockwold-cum-Wilton, then first left onto Mill Drift, another trail section. Go right after 2.5 kilometres on the drove to Weeting, then join the road, and turn right, then left, onto All Saints. This takes you past Weeting Castle, a ruined medieval manor. The metalled road merges into an off-road track at Holme Farm. Follow this track to the A1065, where you turn right, then first left, onto a long, straight lane with trees either side. Take care here: the track is rutted and has potholes in places.

Cross the A134 at Lynford, again with care, then take the first left and follow this off-road section to a crossroads of trails, where you go right. Turn left on the A134, then first right onto a narrow lane, and take the first trail right after Field Barn. Follow this sandy trail, called Harling Grove, west to the A1065, then turn left to Brandon.

4

The South and West

8 Wiltshire Droves
Exploring the historic roads of the lovely South Wiltshire Downs

DIFFICULTY RATING **7/10** WILDNESS RATING **7/10**

Drovers' roads were built for collecting livestock and driving it to market with dogs by men called drovers. Many drovers' roads became part of the road network we use today, but where they exist in their near-original state they access some of Britain's wildest places. They are really special for cyclists because, built by local people, they followed the contours and took the paths of least resistance, which makes them perfect for pedalling.

The history of drovers' roads stretches back centuries, but in some remote places they were used for their original purpose until quite recently. When I recced route number 45 for this book, Border Reiver, I met a man whose father was a drover as recently as the 1960s. He would herd a hundred sheep, using two dogs, and drive them along to the local railhead, which every market town had before Richard Beeching axed most of them during his stint as chairman of British Railways. This Northumberland drover was away from home for up to a week, walking 10 to 12 miles a day with his sheep. It was a life very different from almost any lived in the UK today.

Drovers' roads are really well preserved, and run for miles on and around the South Wiltshire Downs between Salisbury and Shaftesbury. This ride uses three of them: two higher routes, one of which, Shaftesbury Drove, runs along an undulating ridge, and a third which links the other two.

It's quite a long ride, with a steep descent and a climb in the middle, but it's straightforward and thoroughly enjoyable: a real chance to get out, see the countryside and live in the

FACT FILE

Where East Camborne Chase area of the South Wiltshire Downs, about 4 kilometres south-west of Salisbury

OS grid ref SU 0928 2550

Start/Finish Salisbury Racecourse

Ride distance 32 kilometres (20 miles)

Highest points Top of Swallowcliffe Down (214 metres), top of Woodminton Down (224 metres)

Approximate time 4–5 hours

moment. The tops of the Wiltshire Downs in particular have such a free, wide-open feel, and glorious views.

I started from Salisbury Racecourse, but the town of Salisbury itself isn't far away, and offers better parking and good transport links. The road leading west from the Racecourse is Shaftesbury Drove. Continue west along the southern edge of a wood called Hare Warren, and ride along the spine of the Downs – first Compton Down, then Fovent, then Sutton and Swallowcliffe Downs. Trees line either side of the trail at first, but they thin out later in places.

The land dips steeply to the north, less so to the south, and the down tops are wide. The views are incredible. Wiltshire has always had strong military connections, and where the trail bends sharp left, below you on Fovent Down, facing north, are the Fovent Badges. These are giant regimental badges carved by soldiers waiting to go and fight in the First World War, and created by removing the grass to reveal the white chalk below. The badges are maintained today by the Fovent Badges Society in memory of the soldiers who made them: www.foventbadges.com.

Continue on Shaftesbury Drove until the second road crossing, where

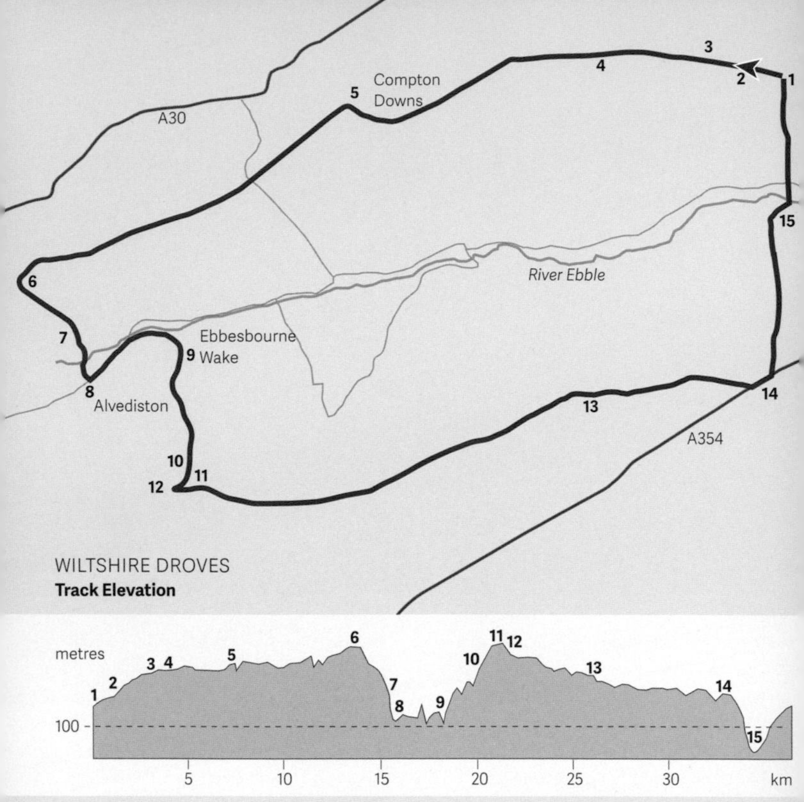

WILTSHIRE DROVES

Track Elevation

1 Start/Finish, Salisbury Racecourse

2 Shaftsbury Drove section starts

3 Hare Warren

4 First of a series of bridleway or byway access/exit points to this ride

5 Fovant Bridges

6 Turn left onto road and descend steeply

7 Steepest downhill, take care

8 Turn left

9 Keep right

10 Steepest uphill

11 Turn left onto Ox Drove

12 Highest point of ride, 223 metres

13 Sharp right then left

14 Left onto main road, then first left

15 Steep descent

you go left. There's a very steep descent: keep your speed within your comfort zone and beware of a very sharp right bend at the bottom, just after passing a church.

Once in Alvediston turn left at the staggered junction and follow the road to Ebbesbourne Wake, where you keep right and begin climbing a hill called the Hollow to the top of Woodminton Down. Alvediston stands at the source of the Ebble, the river that carved out the valley you are riding around. It's a charming, babbling chalk stream, with crystal-clear water that feeds a watercress farm further down the valley.

Turn left at the top of Woodminton Down and follow the road on to Ox Drove. Shaftesbury Drove can get bumpy, but Ox Drove is far more cut-up, so it's rough in places. It's still glorious, though, with fewer trees lining it, so you get more opportunities to take in the fabulous views.

This section of Ox Drove crosses several roads, each of which gives access to the Ebble Valley, from where, should you want to cut this ride short, you can head back to Salisbury Racecourse. There's one sharp right turn, after which you go almost immediately sharp left, on Ox Drove. Don't forget, because if you continue right you'll enter private land.

Eventually the trail joins the A354, where you go left onto the main road for 300 metres, then take the first trail left. This undulates for a couple of kilometres to the top of Throope Hill, then plunges down to the village of Stratford Tony. Take care descending – it's rough in places – and go right where the trail forks. In Stratford Tony the trail turns into road: go straight at the crossroads and continue uphill back to the start.

9 Winfrith Riot

Exploring the drove roads of Dorset along the edge of the Purbeck Heritage Coast

DIFFICULTY RATING **7/10** WILDNESS RATING **6/10**

The worst thing you can say about this ride is that it starts at the bottom of a long, steep hill. However, the view from the top is magnificent, and the rest of the ride is splendid. It's a mix of coast and country, with an overwhelming feel of freedom and little bits of history thrown in.

Lulworth Cove has a car park at its visitor centre, but there is also the possibility of street parking in West Lulworth. Visit Lulworth Cove before you start, because aesthetically and geologically it is one of the finest examples of a cove anywhere in the world. It formed here because bands of rock with different levels of resistance run parallel to the coast, and the sea eroded the softer rocks behind the cliffs more than the cliffs themselves, thereby hollowing out a perfect cove.

Turning your back on the sea, ride uphill from Lulworth Cove and, on entering West Lulworth, take the left fork towards Daggers Gate. This takes you to the top of the hill, where you go left on Daggers Gate Road, which quickly becomes a trail.

Follow this undulating trail west, taking time to appreciate the sea views to the south, for 4 kilometres, to a junction near the National Trust land around Burning Cliff. Here you join a road: keep right, and then where a trail called Falcon Barn forks left, go right. Follow the road north past Holworth village, and turn right on the trail at the top of the next hill, Gallow's Hill. Gallow's Hill is said to be haunted, but then, according to local legend, most of Dorset is.

Stay on the trail, which follows hedgerows and the ridgeline, all the way to Winfrith Newburgh, an idyllic

FACT FILE

Where The Purbeck Heritage Coast runs from the Isle of Purbeck west to Weymouth, south of the A352 Dorchester-to-Wareham road

OS grid ref SY 8243 7992

Start/Finish Lulworth Cove

Ride distance 22 kilometres (13.75 miles)

Highest point On Dagger's Gate Road, 5.24 kilometres into the ride

Approximate time 3–4 hours

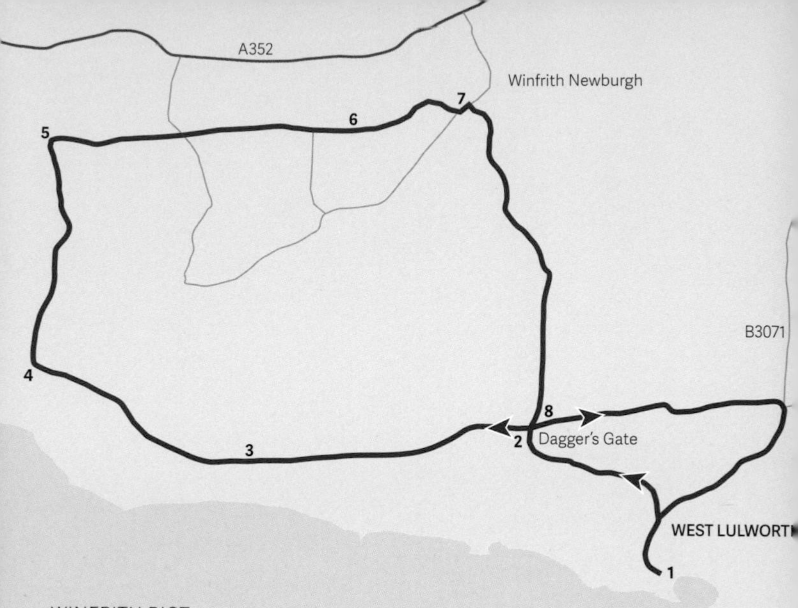

WINFRITH RIOT

Track Elevation

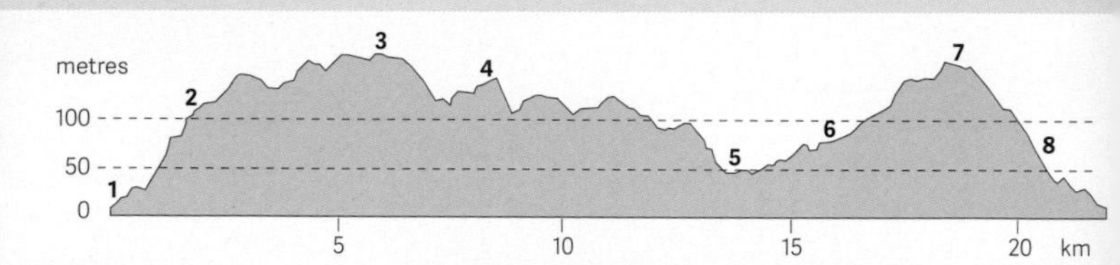

1 Start/Finish
2 Turn left onto Dagger's Gate trail west going out
3 Highest point
4 Burning Cliff, turn right
5 Gallows Hill, turn right onto trail
6 Follow trail along ridge line
7 Turn left, then first right
8 Turn left onto Dagger's Gate trail east coming back

peaceful Dorset village nowadays, but in November 1830 the scene of a riot. At least, it's recorded as a riot: in fact it was a peaceful protest by agricultural workers against low wages.

They failed to disperse when asked to by the local magistrate, James Frampton, who then read them the Riot Act. That didn't work, so with 150 special constables he charged the crowd, arresting three men. They were dealt with quite leniently for the time, and Frampton later noted that the protestors were 'generally fine-looking men who appeared to be in their Sunday best'.

Stay on the trail, which follows hedgerows and the ridgeline, all the way to Winfrith Newburgh, an idyllic peaceful Dorset village nowadays, but in November 1830 the scene of a riot.

Turn left in Winfrith, then go first right past St Christopher's Church, and follow this road south through a lovely steep-sided valley to Daggers Gate. Go left there, and follow the trail to Lulworth Camp. Turn right, and ride back through West Lulworth to the start.

10 Mendip Meander
Through, round and across the wonderful Mendip Hills

DIFFICULTY RATING **7/10** WILDNESS RATING **6/10**

The Mendips are a chain of limestone hills south of Bristol that stretch from the Bristol Channel at Weston-Super-Mare 45 kilometres inland to Frome. They're a great place for wild cycling, with a network of tiny lanes and bridleways going up and down and across the hills.

I used a typical selection of them for this ride, plus part of Sustrans, or National Cycle Network (NCN), route 26, which is where our Mendip Meander starts. When it is finished, route 26 will eventually run from Portishead to Portland Bill, so from the Bristol to the English Channel. The section this ride uses is converted from a railway known as the Strawberry Line. It provides a nice gentle start, because there are some steep hills and bumpy trails later. It's a ride for a cyclo-cross, gravel or mountain bike.

I chose Winscombe as the place to pick up the trail, but don't go on May Day because the former station, where this rides starts, hosts the town's May Day Fair. Head south on the old railway line, past the King's Wood car park, which would make an alternative start, to Axbridge, where navigation gets a bit tricky. As the trail approaches a road the trail goes right and runs next to the road, but becomes much less distinct. Don't ride down the road, because it's one-way, with traffic coming in the opposite direction.

The trail joins West Street in Axbridge, which becomes High Street, then St Mary's, and eventually Cheddar Road. Basically, just follow the main drag through Axbridge. Eventually you approach the A371: look for an NCN route 26 sign on your right to continue on the Strawberry Line to Cheddar.

FACT FILE

Where This ride is 20 kilometres south-west of central Bristol, and the same north-east of Bridgwater, about 10 kilometres from junction 21 of the M5

OS grid ref ST 4190 5763

Start/Finish Winscombe old railway station

Ride distance 31.5 kilometres (19.7 miles)

Highest point Beacon Batch (325 metres)

Approximate time 3–4 hours

Once in Cheddar, on reaching Sharpham Road go left, then left again on Lower New Road, and right onto Wildeats Road. Follow this as it becomes Station Road, then go left on Union Street and left again on Cliff Road. This leads to Cheddar Gorge, and an incredible cycling experience.

Cycling up Cheddar Gorge is difficult, but pure joy. Blast your way up if you like, but it's better to select your lowest gear and marvel at this cathedral of rock. The cliffs at the entrance rise 130 metres above you. What force must the Ice Age meltwater that carved out this deep gash in the limestone have had?

Cycling up Cheddar Gorge is difficult, but pure joy. Blast your way up if you like, but it's better to select your lowest gear and marvel at this cathedral of rock. The cliffs at the entrance rise 130 metres above you.

But Cheddar Gorge is not just geology and landscape: it played a crucial role in human history, when its caves were home to some of the very first settlements. In 1903 a complete skeleton from one of Cheddar's caves was found to be 9,000 years old, while other human bone fragments found

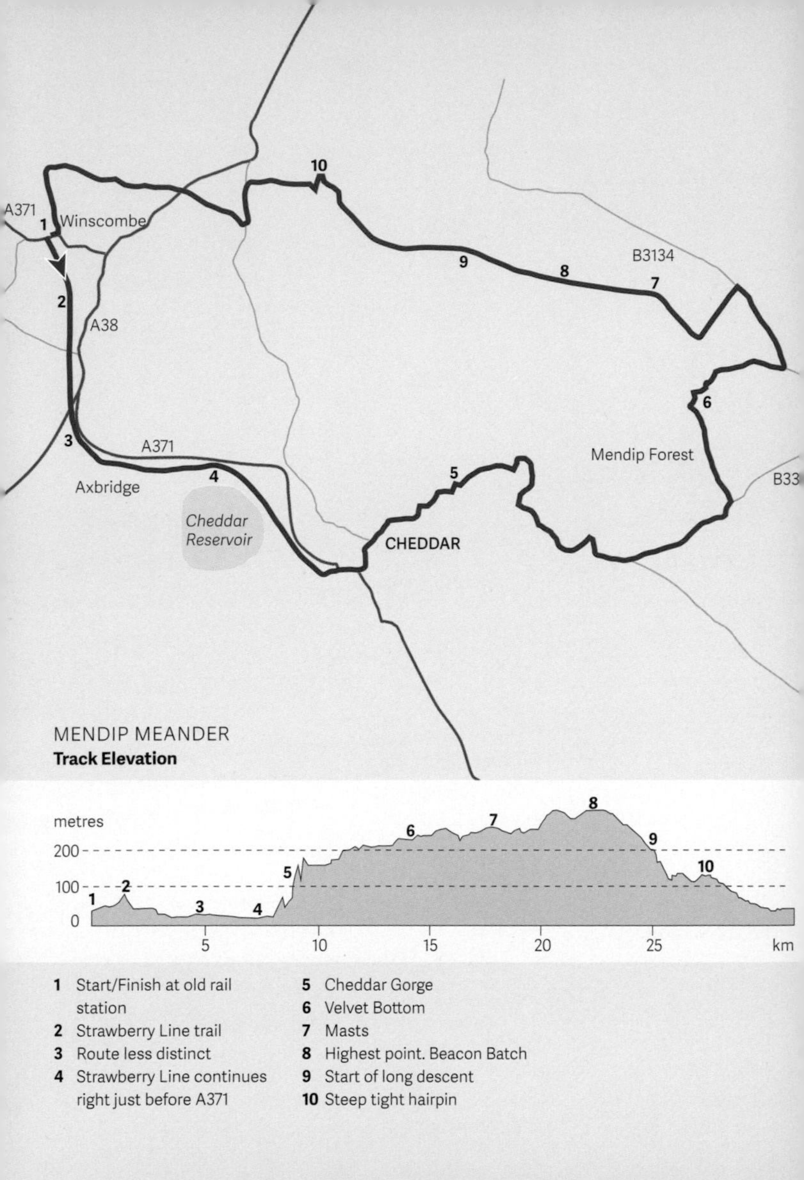

A371
1
Winscombe
10
2
A38
9
8
B3134
7
6
3
A371
4
Axbridge
Cheddar
Reservoir
5
CHEDDAR
Mendip Forest
B33
MENDIP MEANDER
Track Elevation
metres
200
100
0
1
2
3
4
5
6
7
8
9
10
5
10
15
20
25
km
1 Start/Finish at old rail station
2 Strawberry Line trail
3 Route less distinct
4 Strawberry Line continues right just before A371
5 Cheddar Gorge
6 Velvet Bottom
7 Masts
8 Highest point. Beacon Batch
9 Start of long descent
10 Steep tight hairpin

here have been dated at 12–13,000 years old. With caves all the way up the rock face, Cheddar Gorge was, you might say, Britain's first tower block.

Carry on out of the gorge, go left at the fork in the road to a crossroads at a farm, where you turn left. Follow the lane into and out of a shallow offshoot of Cheddar Gorge called Velvet Bottom, and turn right to follow a road that becomes a trail to the B3134.

Turn left and follow the road for a kilometre, then go left and then first right. This is a little lane called Rains Batch that goes uphill to some radio masts. Go left at the masts onto a bridleway for a long off-road section across Black Down, the roof of the Mendips. The trail is bumpy and rutted in places, but the open landscape looks wonderful. During the Second World War a decoy was built up here designed to simulate the lights of a town, in the hope of confusing enemy bombers and protecting Bristol.

Ignore any side trails, although it's worth deviating north near the summit of the bridleway to visit Beacon Batch, the highest hill in the Mendips. A trail takes you to Beacon Batch and back onto this route. Once back, continue north-west and you enter a coniferous woodland called Rowberrow Warren.

Ignore the first side trails in the woods, then go right where the bridleway forks. You start going downhill quite steeply from here, so take care. Follow what is more like a fire road, keeping left at a junction where there's a clearing on your right. Soon you reach a very steep and tight left-hand hairpin bend: take great care. About 100 metres out of the bend the bridleway joins the junction of School Lane and Back Lane. Go right on School Lane.

Follow School Lane to the T-junction with Rowberrow Lane, and go straight across it onto the last bridleway section. Follow this to New Road, where you turn left to Shipham. Go right at the first crossroads in Shipham to Broadway. Cross the busy A38 at Star, and the next junction is at the north end of Winscombe. Turn left and ride back to where you started.

11 Dartmoor Snapshot
Exploring some of the tors and rivers of north Dartmoor

DIFFICULTY RATING **8/10** WILDNESS RATING **7/10**

Dartmoor is a great wild-cycling destination. There are trails all over the moor, so you can get close-up to its striking tors, which stick like bones of rock through Dartmoor's thin skin, and even get your wheels wet in its boisterous rivers. The little lanes that play around the edge of Dartmoor are a joy, too. On this ride, located at the northern edge of the moor, you experience both.

It's quite arduous, but it's not long, and you are never far from civilisation. The start is in Meldon Reservoir car park. First, go left out of the car park to ride across Meldon Dam. The view into the West Okement valley is fabulous. You get another glimpse of it when you cross a viaduct, and the ride finishes with a very steep pull up from the valley back to the car park.

Once you've soaked up the view, double back towards Meldon village. Go right after the first house and you'll see an old railway bridge, crossed by the Granite Way, an 11-mile cycle trail running from Okehampton to Lydford.

Join the Granite Way and follow it eastwards. Going west would take you to Lydford and Lydford Gorge, which, if you've time, is really worth seeing. The Granite Way also makes a great family ride, because there are no gradients, but great swathes of Dartmoor beauty all the way.

Back on this ride follow the Granite Way across the viaduct, then alongside a heritage railway, and under the A30 until you pass under Tors Road, which climbs out of Okehampton and onto Dartmoor. The Granite Way doubles back on itself here to form a T-junction with Tors Road. For this ride turn right onto Tors Road, but you could turn left and miss out the next section, because in 2 kilometres there's a ferociously steep off-road climb and a rough section

FACT FILE

Where Okehampton is 22 miles west of Exeter along the A30

OS grid ref SX 5611 9175

Start/Finish Meldon Reservoir car park

Ride distance 23.6 kilometres (14.75 miles)

Highest point Just below Rowtor (416 metres)

Approximate time 2.5–3.5 hours

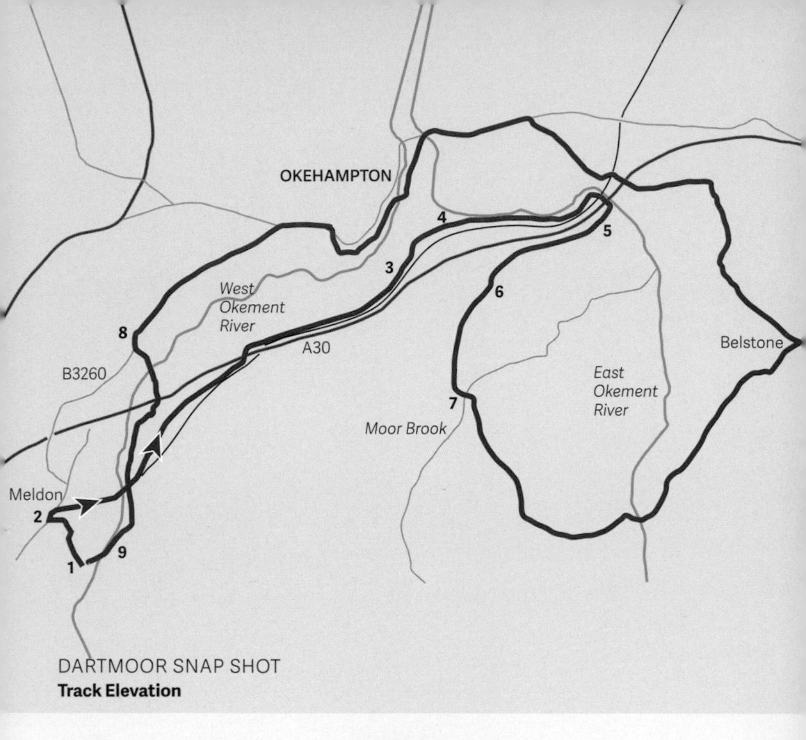

DARTMOOR SNAP SHOT

Track Elevation

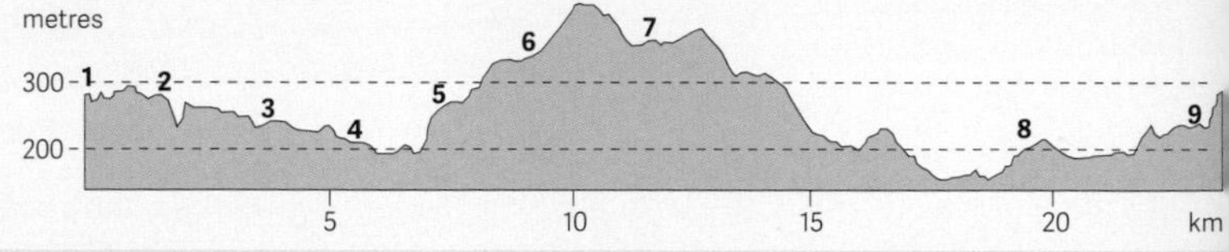

1. Start/Finish
2. Join Granite Way
3. Turn left on Tors Road
4. Right on Parkland and join bridleway
5. Very steep hill
6. Join road
7. Army Camp
8. Left onto lane
9. Very steep hill to car park

of trail. It's quite demanding, but if you are undaunted it's a great experience.

So, if you've opted for the full ride, descend towards Okehampton, then take the next right, called Parklands. Ride along this street, then pick up a bridleway that starts to the left of the entrance to Okehampton Station, the base of the heritage railway. There's a great café on the station platform.

The bridleway continues east through some trees above Okehampton for just over a kilometre, before turning sharp right at the East Okement River. You ride under the heritage railway line, then under the A30, which rumbles eerily overhead on a flyover supported by massive concrete pillars. Turn right as soon you emerge from the flyover.

This is the ferocious off-road climb. The surface is loose, so powerful but at the same time sensitive pedalling is required to get up it without walking. It's not long, and walking is no shame. Once at the top you follow a lumpy trail parallel to the A30, which runs almost directly beneath you.

After a kilometre look for another trail on your left that climbs diagonally across the side of East Hill. This trail joins Tors Road at a hairpin bend. Turn left at the hairpin and follow the road to Okehampton Army Camp. Go left at the camp, and continue climbing to a pass between Rowtor on the right and a slightly lower un-named peak on the left. A word of caution here: all the

It's quite arduous, but it's not long, and you are never far from civilisation.

roads around the army camp are part of a military range, so before you do this ride you must check that there is no military activity planned for the day. Use this link: http://www.dartmoor-ranges.co.uk/firing_notice_1.html

The pass is followed by a steep descent to a collection of stones called Cullever Steps, which provides a shallow way across the East Okement River. The steps aren't really suitable for crossing by bike, but luckily there's a bridge as well. Just downstream of Cullever Steps there's a deep swimming hole in the river, which is well known to wild swimming devotees. On a nice warm day, what could be better than a quick wild swim in the middle of a wild ride?

Once across Cullever Steps there's a choice of trails. Take the left fork, and head north-west around Scary Tor and into Belstone. There are lots more trails to explore around this delightful old Devon village, especially near Belstone Cleave. Head west from Belstone to South Zeal and you can climb back up onto Dartmoor using a number of bridleways. For this ride, though, go left in the centre of Belstone and head for Okehampton.

After passing under the A30 and the railway bridge, go left on Fartherford

Road, which leads up to the town. Turn left on Exeter Road, descend into Okehampton and take the second left after the church, called Mill Road. This leads to Simmons Park, which is one of the best civic spaces I've ever seen. Manicured grass and well-tended gardens are backed by steep woodland and the beginnings of Dartmoor. Above the wood a shelf of land holds the A30, the railway and the bridleway you rode out to Dartmoor on earlier. The park is well used by Okehamptoners, who are justifiably proud of it.

Go left out of the park, continuing along Mill Road, then take the second left, Castle Road. This becomes Castle Lane after crossing the West Okement River, where you start the long climb past the ruin of Okehampton Castle, often painted, notably by J. M. W. Turner. Keep climbing, and you come out on the B3260. Turn left onto it and keep climbing for another 2 kilometres, then go left opposite the Betty Cottles pub onto a narrow lane that rises steeply across the A30.

The road flattens as you ride through a small wood and under the Granite Way viaduct you rode across earlier. Carry straight on where the road swings left to Meldon Quarry to pick up a bridleway. The trail then forks: keep left of the small pond, another notable wild swimming location, and you are faced with the last steep uphill climb to the car park. Give it the beans.

12 Exmoor Experience
A sample of what mighty Exmoor has for off-the-beaten-track rides

DIFFICULTY RATING **7/10** WILDNESS RATING **8/10**

Exmoor is a high, wide dome of land that rises out of the Bristol Channel and undulates gently across Devon and Somerset towards Tarka Country, the Devon valleys of the Rivers Taw and Torridge. There are so many rideable trails here it's hard to choose, while the really dramatic coastline is edged by tiny roads and bits of trail.

Riding the coastal trails and lanes, particularly around Woody Bay just west of Lynton, is something you should try one day. A warning though: some places are exposed, and the drops are scary. For this ride I've gone inland to try a mix of moorland and valley, in a circuit around the young River Exe.

I started in Exford. From the B3224 in the village a road runs north-west. Follow it and take the first right, Combe Lane. Carry straight on where this becomes the Samaritans Way South-West, then go left after 1,200 metres onto a little road. Go left again, then right and immediately left. Follow this lane, continuing when it becomes a trail across Almsworthy Common. Halfway along this section you pass a group of 14 standing stones on your right, which are thought to be the work of humans in prehistoric times.

Turn left when you get to a road, then go straight onto a trail section where the road bends sharply left. The trail flows the contours around two low hills to Warren Farm, where it becomes a road again. Follow this downhill into Exe Cleve, where the infant River Exe flows. Cross the Exe and climb out up the other side of the valley.

For the next bit you go right on the B3224 and descend to Simonsbath. Just before the bridge over the River Barle there's a trail going off to the

FACT FILE

Where Exford is a village at the heart of the Exmoor National Park, 16 kilometres (10 miles) south-east of Minehead

OS grid ref SS 8536 3842

Start/Finish Exford

Ride distance 26 kilometres (16.25 miles)

Highest point Halfway across Almsworthy Common (437 metres)

Approximate time 2–3 hours

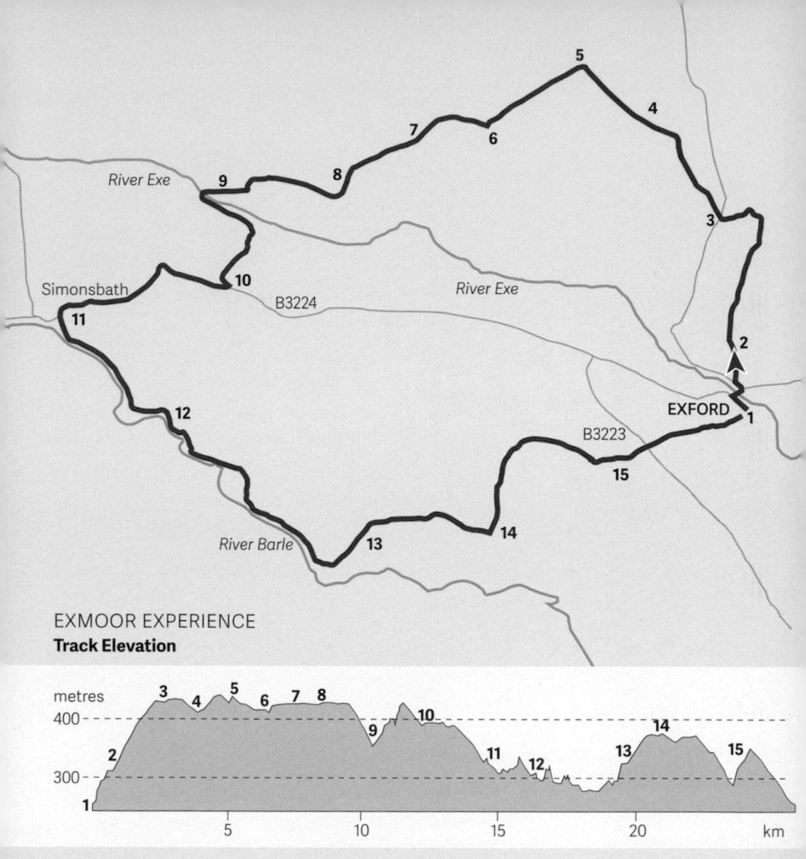

1 Start/Finish

2 Steep uphill first two kilometres

3 Right then left onto trail

4 Standing stones

5 Left onto road

6 Right onto trail where road bends sharp left

7 Keep left where trail forks

8 This section of trail is rough in places

9 Steep down then uphill

10 Turn right to Simonsbath

11 Turn left before bridge onto Two Moors Way

12 Trail rough in places

13 Steep uphill

14 Turn left onto road

15 Steep uphill

Riding the coastal trails and lanes, particularly around Woody Bay just west of Lynton, is something you should try one day. A warning though: some places are exposed, and the drops are scary.

right. This is the Two Moors Way: follow it down the Barle Valley, riding alongside the river for much of the way. It's a really delightful section of the ride, but rough in places.

Just over one kilometre after a mound called Cow Castle, the remains of an Iron-Age fort, the trail leaves the Barle and goes uphill, eventually reaching a moorland road. Turn left on the road and follow it, crossing the B3223, all the way back to Exford. Like all the rides in this book, this one isn't definitive. There are lots of variations you could throw in, and similar rides all over Exmoor.

13 Wheels within Wheals

A Cornish industrial heritage ride, made up of lanes, trails and converted tramways of old metal mines

DIFFICULTY RATING **6/10** WILDNESS RATING **7/10**

Cornwall hasn't always been idyllic beaches, surf sun and seagulls. Two hundred years ago it was a hive of noisy industry, and many of the county's rivers and beaches, and much of its landscape, were a toxic mess. Cornwall was rich, though, or at least its landowners were, making money from fishing and in particular from mining. But both industries inflicted an environmental cost it has taken years to claim back.

When mining was at its height, from Redruth westwards and on parts of Bodmin Moor, nothing could be heard but the clank of metal and hiss of steam. Engines powered the winding houses that hauled various ores, in particular tin and copper, to the surface, and the pumps that prevented the pits flooding. There were hundreds of large and small private mines. You can still see their skeletons and tottering chimneys today. They were linked by a network of railway lines, which in turn linked them to the sea, so imported coal could be hauled inland to fuel the engines, and metal could be hauled out for export. Many of these old lines, which were called tramways, have been converted into paths for cyclists and walkers, and this ride uses them extensively.

There are over 60 kilometres of cycle trails in Cornwall that used to be tramways. Most have hard surfaces, and in a hilly county most are comparatively flat. You can link them together for a big ride, or use them to go coast-to-coast, 12 miles each way from Devoran to Portreath. Short sections of the trails make perfect family rides. This ride uses some of the coast-to-coast route, and an interesting loop around the old mines, or wheals, as they were called in Cornwall.

The ride starts in Devoran at the

FACT FILE

Where Cornwall, in the middle of a triangle formed by Truro, Falmouth and Redruth

OS grid ref SW 7971 3897

Start/Finish Devoran

Ride distance 15 kilometres (9.4 miles)

Highest point Trail summit after Twelveheads (115 metres)

Approximate time 2 hours

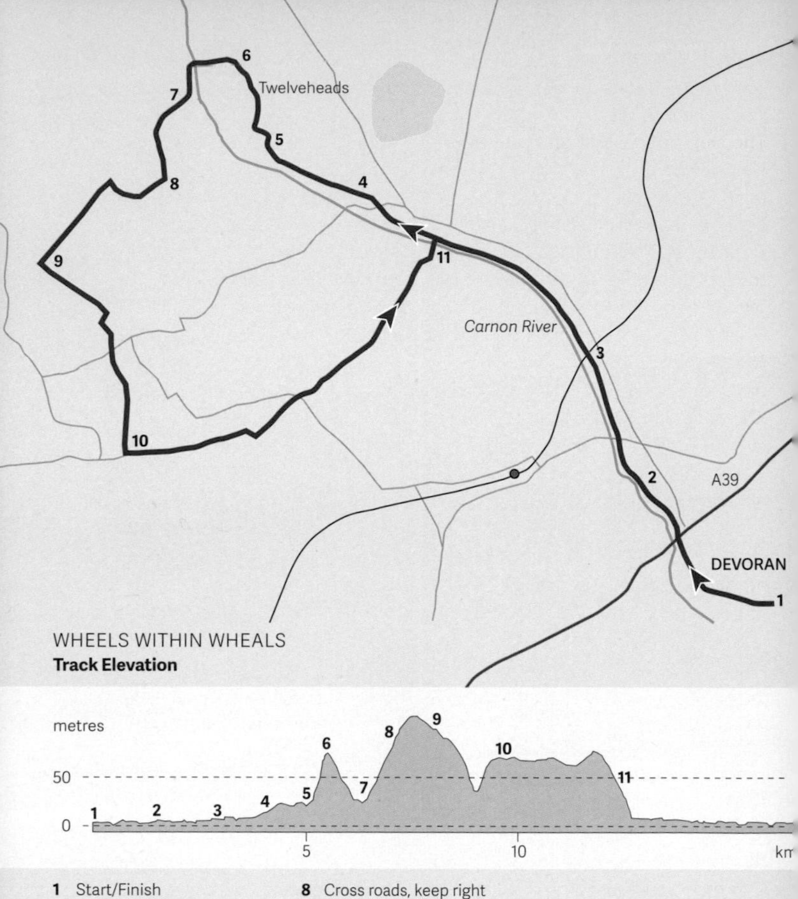

1. **1** Start/Finish
2. **2** Carnon Mine
3. **3** Viaduct and Brunel Stumps
4. **4** Bike Chain Bissoe Bike Hire and Café
5. **5** Keep right and on uphill for Twelveheads
6. **6** Turn left onto road
7. **7** Go straight on to the trail at the road T-junction
8. **8** Cross roads, keep right then turn left
9. **9** Left turn here then across next two roads
10. **10** Left turn onto road
11. **11** Turn right for bike trail back to start, of left for café

head of Restronguet Creek, one of several mysterious Cornish tidal-ways that open into the English Channel. The most famous is Helford River just west of Falmouth, which is reputed to be haunted and is the location for Daphne du Maurier's famous novel, *Frenchman's Creek*. Devoran used to be the southern railhead and quay for this section of the Cornish mining industry.

The route leaves Devoran by road, passing a village hall that used to be the locomotive workshop. The first mine, Carnon Mine, is only a few hundred metres inland, and it's a very old one that used an equally old method of mining. Carnon was a stream mine, which worked on effectively the same principle the old prospectors used when panning for gold. People have found metal ore in this way for centuries. In Truro museum there's a nugget of gold on display that archaeologists reckon was found in this part of the Carnon River during the Bronze Age. However, stream mines like Carnon were panning on an industrial scale that involved digging shafts down into the silt, hauling it out and sifting through it up on the surface.

Follow Carnon River upstream and you ride under an impressive viaduct across the valley. It carries the railway line to Falmouth, but just to the north of it you'll find the Brunel Stumps, eleven stone piers that remain from Isambard Kingdom Brunel's original Carnon viaduct. Brunel built wooden trestles on top of the piers to carry the railway line, but the piers' foundations weren't up to carrying modern trains, so a new viaduct was built.

Tin and copper weren't the only things mined in the Carnon Valley, as the next chimney along the trail reveals. It belonged to Point Mills arsenic refinery, and Cornwall was once the world centre for arsenic production. This poisonous mineral was used in many industrial processes, including glass-making, and in early insecticides.

Arsenic added to Cornwall's post-industrial pollution problems, and long after land sites were cleaned, many streams, although crystal-clear, were only like that because of the arsenic they contained, which meant no life could survive in them. But things are getting better: one recently developed clean-up process involves planting ferns, which convert arsenic into a non-poisonous compound.

Continue past the arsenic works, cross two roads, and then the trail passes Bike Chain Bissoe Bike Hire and café. This is a great place with great food, run by a real cycling enthusiast, Richard Pascoe. He's stuffed the café full of memorabilia, including jerseys, flags and photographs signed by Olympic champions and Tour de France winners.

As you continue on the trail you'll encounter a profusion of old mine

buildings, and chimneys sprouting out of the woods all the way up the hillsides. Millions of years ago molten lava intruded into this region's underlying sedimentary rock, and the subsequent heat and pressure caused metals such as zinc, tin, copper, gold and silver to concentrate into lodes, which is why there was so much mining in this area.

Turn second right after the power lines, and climb the hill to Twelveheads, a village named after a machine used to crush ore there, which had 12 hammerheads. From here you could continue north to Cornwall's Atlantic coast at Portreath, or you could ride an extra couple of miles to Chacewater, where the Wheal Busy mine is. One of James Watt's first steam engines was installed here. Cornwall was a crucible for industrial innovation. Sir Humphrey Davy, who in 1815 invented the miner's safety lamp, was Cornish. The lamp detected poisonous gases, and represented such a quantum jump in safety that a version is still in use today.

For this ride you go left, then descend to the T-junction just south of Twelveheads. Go straight across the T-junction and onto a trail. Cross the next road, keep right, then turn left and, after a kilometre, left again. Follow this trail south-east, then south, crossing two roads, then turn left on the Pulla Cross-to-Frogpool road and follow it north-east back to the Carnon Valley trail. Turn right to retrace your outward journey back to Devoran, or left for the Bike Chain Bissoe café if you fancy a drink and a bite to eat. Once back in Devoran, if you still want more cycling, a lovely ride is to be had following the road that hugs the estuary all the way to Restronguet Point on the Carrick Roads inlet.

5

Wales

14 Caerphilly Classic

A mix of lanes and trails across the hills between Cardiff and Caerphilly and along the Rhymney Valley

DIFFICULTY RATING **7/10** WILDNESS RATING **5/10**

I didn't call this ride the Caerphilly Classic because it's a classic wild ride, although it's interesting and pretty wild in places: I called it Classic because parts of it were shown to me by the Welsh pro racer Luke Rowe, and he's a key man in Team Sky's Classics race campaign.

Classics are rugged and very selective single-day races, and this ride is rugged in places, too. Rowe stuck to the metalled lanes when he showed it to me, and I've added some off-road sections – shortcuts, really. Having said that, some of Rowe's lanes are pretty gnarly.

Rowe used his time-trial bike when showing me the bones of the ride, its only adaptation to rough conditions being a pair of robust tyres and training wheels. His choice of bike was a pro racer thing: they don't get many opportunities to ride their special time-trial bikes, so they try to snatch ride hours whenever and wherever possible. A time-trial bike looks incongruous in the hilly, wet lanes of South Wales, but it backs up my argument that you can enjoy some degree of wild cycling on almost any kind of bike.

I started the ride in Lisvane, a posh northern suburb of Cardiff where lots of Cardiff City footballers live. From Lisvane and Thornhill railway station head east on Cherry Orchard Road, go straight on at the roundabout, then left on Graig Road at the T-junction. This goes uphill, over the M4, then gets progressively steeper until a brutal last 200 metres. To pace your effort, remember that the steepest bit starts where you go under some electricity pylons.

The road bends sharp right at the top of the hill, then sharp left, then it plunges downwards. Take care here:

FACT FILE

Where North Cardiff; access from junction 30 of the M4

OS grid ref ST 1792 8352

Start/Finish Thornhill and Lisvane railway station

Ride distance 23.5 kilometres (14.7 miles)

Highest points Graig Road Hill (243 metres), Caerphilly Mountain (249 metres)

Approximate time 2–3 hours

you go through a short section of trees, out into the open, then into more trees, and the road then bends sharp left in the trees, with the first trail section, a bridleway, on your right. It's best to come to a complete stop before turning onto the trail so you can check for vehicles behind or coming up the hill towards you. When it's safe to do so, turn right onto the trail.

The first section is quite distinct and reasonably smooth, because it's also the drive to a cottage, but after 500 metres the trail goes through thick forest and in places is quite green and bumpy. An alternative would be to continue descending the road you were on and go right at the T-junction. This would take you to where the off-road option comes out opposite the Maenllwyd Inn. If you've arrived at Maenllwyd Inn by the trail, turn left, then go right to Rudry; if you choose the road option, take the first left.

In Rudry go right at the primary school, and keep right, following a narrow lane to Machen. Enter the town by Green Row, which runs alongside the Rhymney River. Go left on Forge Road, left on the main Commercial Road, and right on Dranllywn Lane. After 100 metres you reach the Rhymney Valley Cycle Path on your left. This is a converted railway

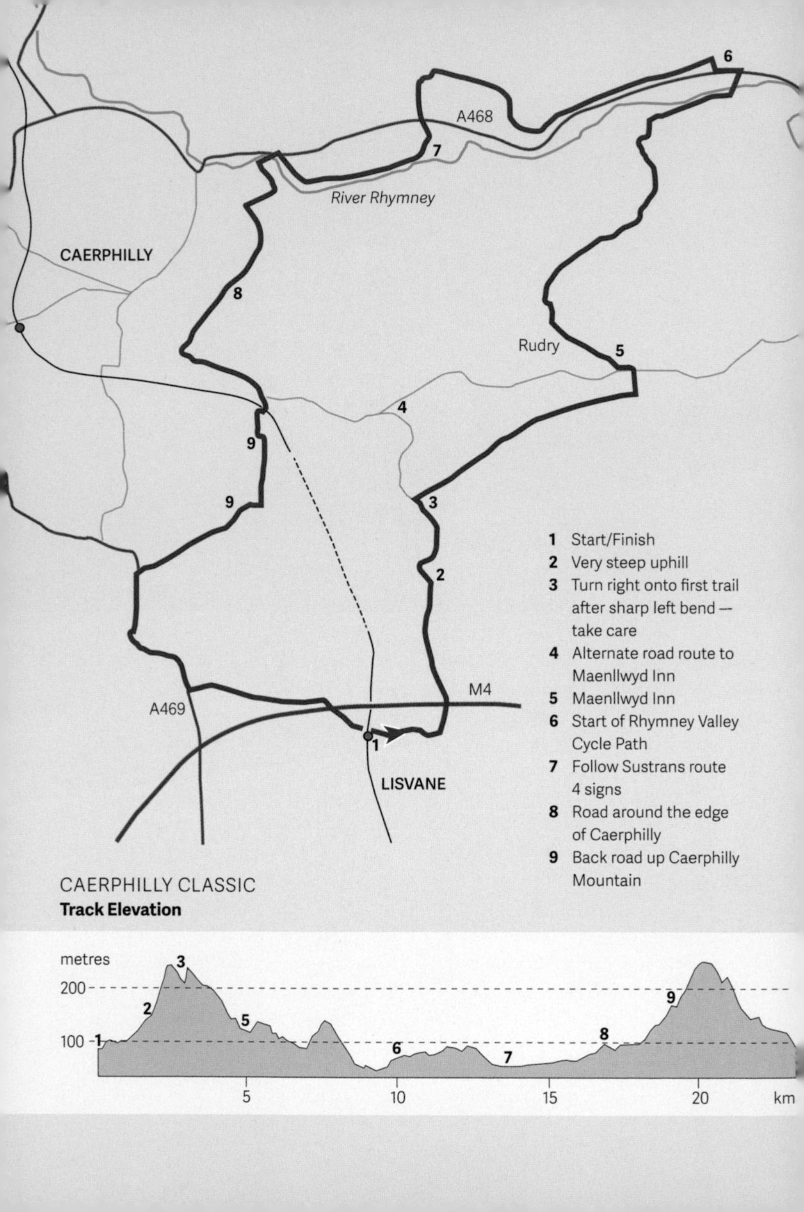
A468
River Rhymney
CAERPHILLY
Rudry
M4
A469
LISVANE
1
2
3
4
5
6
7
8
9
9
1 Start/Finish
2 Very steep uphill
3 Turn right onto first trail after sharp left bend — take care
4 Alternate road route to Maenllwyd Inn
5 Maenllwyd Inn
6 Start of Rhymney Valley Cycle Path
7 Follow Sustrans route 4 signs
8 Road around the edge of Caerphilly
9 Back road up Caerphilly Mountain
CAERPHILLY CLASSIC
Track Elevation
metres
200
100
5
10
15
20
km

line that once carried wrought iron from Machen, which was made from ore mined in the surrounding hills using coal from local mines.

You are now in one of the famous South Wales Valleys; iron steel and coal were produced all along the Rhymney River, which didn't carve all of its deep valley; that was done by glaciers during successive Ice Ages.

Head west on the Rhymney Valley Path, which is part of NCN route 4, so look for route 4 signs to help navigate the next section through Trethomas to the Rhymney River, then cross it and go left on Bedwas Road. The next section takes you left onto Rudry Road, then right, then left onto a road that runs around the south-east edge of Caerphilly, the birthplace of comedian and magician Tommy Cooper, and of Caerphilly Cheese.

Caerphilly is separated from Cardiff by Caerphilly Mountain, which has hosted stage finishes in the Tour of Britain bike race. In 2012 the Rowe family were out in force here to cheer Luke to fifth place on the stage. The race used the B4263 Mountain Road from the centre of Caerphilly to the top, not the little wild track Rowe uses in training, which is part of this ride.

To find that little track you leave the road going around the edge of Caerphilly by taking the first exit on the Van Road roundabout. Then, after 700 metres, you go right on Cefn Carnau Lane to start climbing the mountain. Follow the tiny track/road, which is rough in places, to the A469, and turn left onto it. Turn left after the steep descent and follow the road back to Thornhill and Lisvane station to complete this ride.

15 Encounter with Offa
A ride through the history and stunning scenery of the Welsh border lands

DIFFICULTY RATING **8/10** WILDNESS RATING **8/10**

In the eighth century, King Offa of Mercia built a fortification between his kingdom and the Kingdom of Powys. It's called Offa's Dyke, and you will meet it several times on this ride, as well as trails dedicated to other historic figures.

The first encounter with Offa happens when you cross the dyke outside Knighton, a border town with a Welsh name as well, Tref-y-Clawd. It wears dual nationality well today, but has seen bloody battles, none worse than when Owain Glyndwr, the last Welsh-born Prince of Wales, laid siege to Knighton's castle in 1402. The first trail you use on this ride is dedicated to Glyndwr, who is a hero in Welsh history.

Glyndwr's Way is a 135-mile footpath, accessible for much of its length to cyclists, running from Knighton northwards to Welshpool. Glyndwr led a Welsh revolt against English occupation throughout the first decade of the 1400s. It was unsuccessful, and he disappeared. Meanwhile his daughter Alys married Sir John Scudamore, the English High Sheriff of Herefordshire. Legend has it that Glyndwr spent the rest of his life in hiding with them as their children's tutor.

That's some of the history; now let's get on with the ride. You pick up Glyndwr's Way on the A4113 just west of Knighton. Go right where the main road bends sharply left, onto a metalled minor road that deteriorates rapidly as you climb Bailey Hill. Keep following the 'Glyndwr' signs.

Bailey Hill top is a wonderful open place, with buzzards and the occasional red kites gliding above. Further west, around Rhyader,

FACT FILE

Where Knighton is on the A4113, halfway between Ludlow and Llandrindod Wells.

OS grid ref SO 2898 7230

Start/Finish Knighton railway station, ample parking nearby.

Ride distance 32 kilometres (20 miles)

Highest points Bailey Hill (400 metres), Llancoch climb (418 metres), Wernygeufron Hill (395 metres), Offa's Dyke on the Jack Mytton Way (420 metres)

Approximate time 4–5 hours

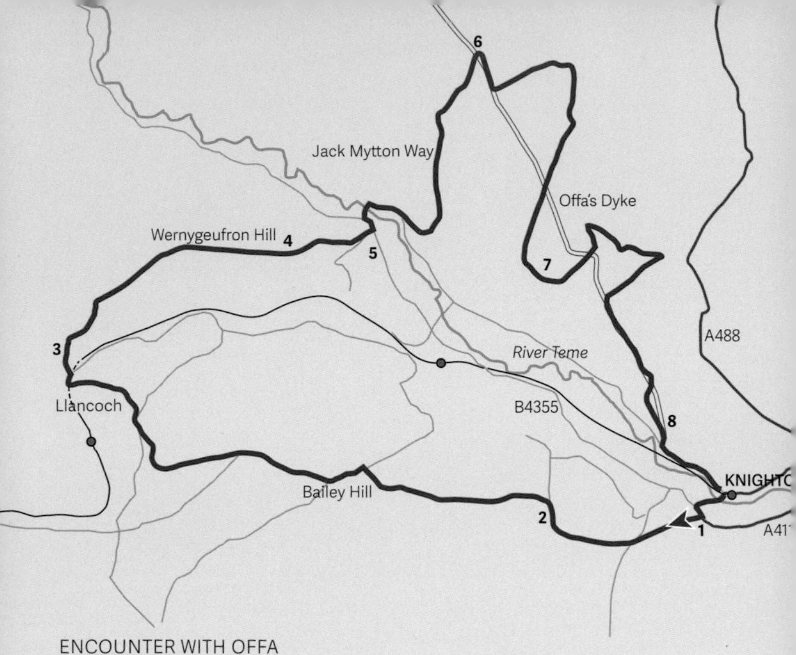

ENCOUNTER WITH OFFA

Track Elevation

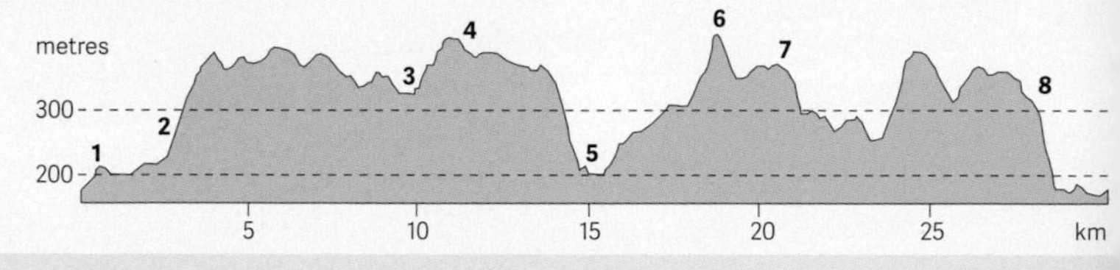

1. Right turn onto Glyndwr's Way
2. Very steep climb
3. Steep climb with steadily worsening surface
4. Rocky descent, slippery under trees
5. Road back to Knighton if short of time or weather worsens
6. The ride's highest point 420 metres
7. Great view
8. Very steep descent

there are many more red kites. In Shakespeare's day they were notorious for stealing underwear, and in King Lear he wrote, 'When kites nest, look to your small linens'. Kites were hunted as vermin, but they never left Wales and, as we saw in the Chilterns, have now been reintroduced in other parts of the UK.

From the top of Bailey Hill, Glyndwr's Way follows a road for a short stretch, then you fork right, following the way-marker signs down to Llancoch. The signs indicate left here, and it's possible to follow Glyndwr's Way for miles by bike, although stretches of footpath increase, making constant cycling impossible. For our route, though, you go right when you hit the road, then first left onto a steep uphill track.

Continue to the summit of Wernygeufron Hill. Several bridleways branch at the top, so follow the one going straight ahead and descend to Lloyney. Take care on this section: the descent is exhilarating, but there are steep bits and drop-offs, especially under the trees at the bottom.

You emerge at the B4355 road. Turn left, then first right. Cross the River Teme, which is the border between Wales and England, then go right at the T-junction and left at a fork in the road. Within 500 metres you come to another junction: continue straight on to a bridleway, which climbs steeply to join the second waymarked trail of this ride, the Jack Mytton Way.

Mytton was a Shropshire landowner, an MP and a thoroughly disreputable character, although in his Regency times the name for a rich gentlemen like him was a rake. Expelled from Westminster and Harrow schools, he gained entry to Cambridge, taking 2,000 bottles of port with him, and left without a degree. His subsequent army career was spent drinking and gambling, and then in 1819 Mytton entered Parliament, giving anyone who voted for him £10. In total his seat cost him £10,000, and Jack's spending and gambling soon became more than his huge estate could support. He ended his days in the debtors' prison, but for such a failure in life he has done well since. There's a pub, a hotel, an annual run and this 72-mile trail all dedicated to him.

The section of the Jack Mytton Way you are on is a long and sometimes rocky climb to a ridge. The ridge is Offa's Dyke, and when you cross through a gap where the earthworks have subsided, you get a glimpse of how it was constructed. Mainly it followed and reinforced natural ridges, with ditches dug where there was no obvious ridge. The dyke can be traced from the Dee estuary down to the River Wye, and all the works to enhance its natural height are on what was the Mercian side, so Mercian guards always looked down on Powys.

A footpath runs along the top

of Offa's Dyke here, so no bikes, but through the gap you come to a bridleway: turn right and follow it for 500 metres until another bridleway goes left. Follow that as it climbs across the face of a hill, then you come to a junction with two more bridleways going right. Follow the second one until just before it becomes a metalled road, then turn right.

This brings you out beside a house. Turn right on the road, but just where the descent suddenly steepens, look to the left, where two tracks leave it. Take the right-hand track and follow this around the contours of Cwm-Sanaham Hill. This is an incredible stretch, with great views over the Teme Valley, but it ends with a savage climb.

At the top, in a small glade of trees, turn right, then go right again on the descent next to a building called New House, and cross the stream. Climb back up to Offa's Dyke. This section of the Dyke has a bridleway on top, so go left and follow it until the trail forks, taking the right-hand fork down to the road leading left into Knighton.

This whole area deserves further exploration. It's called the Welsh Marches now, after the old March of Wales, which until the 14th century was an almost independent country, created to act as a buffer between England and Wales. Today it's a lovely piece of unspoilt rural Britain, and Knighton has a spider's web of rideable connected trails radiating out from it.

16 Idris's Elbow

A mostly off-road ride up onto the shoulders of mighty Cadair Idris

DIFFICULTY RATING **8/10** WILDNESS RATING **8/10**

Cadair Idris is a mountain at the southern end of Snowdonia. In Welsh it means Idris's Chair, Idris probably being Idris Gawr, or Idris the Giant, whose real name was Idris ap Gwydnno, a seventh-century Welsh prince who won a battle against the Irish on this mountain. Idris's Elbow explores the south-west arm of Cadair Idris, which stretches towards the sea at Barmouth Bay.

The ride uses country lanes and old farm tracks, and is suitable for cyclo-cross, gravel bikes and mountain bikes. It starts close to the centre of Llwyngwril. Go south on the A493, and take the first left after the church.

FACT FILE

Where Llwyngwril is on the Merionethshire coast at the southern end of Barmouth Bay, 11 miles south-west of Dolgellau

OS grid ref SH 5912 0593

Start/Finish Llwyngwril centre

Ride distance 27 kilometres (16.9 miles)

Highest point Top of the pass near Craig Cwm Llwyd outcrops (408 metres)

Approximate time 4–5 hours

This road goes steeply uphill for the first 500 metres, but then the gradient lessens. The road surface deteriorates the higher you climb, and there are gates to open and close. This is already a tough ride.

Descend to Rhoslefain – there are more gates to contend with, so be careful – and go left on the A493. It's only for 2 kilometres, and necessary to reach the next section of the ride. Go left to Llanegryn, in the fabulous Dysynni Valley, which further up is part of the Mach Loop, where fast jets regularly do low-level training. Take the first left after Llanegryn to begin the second long climb of this ride.

This trail acts as a pass between several 400- and 500-metre peaks. It's 7 kilometres long, and takes you from 16 metres above sea-level in the valley to over 400 metres above at its summit. It's a very long but incredibly beautiful slog up a quiet valley, to a striking area of lonely hills.

Keep going north-east, then north to the summit, which comes shortly after passing a conifer plantation. The descent is fairly straight, so not

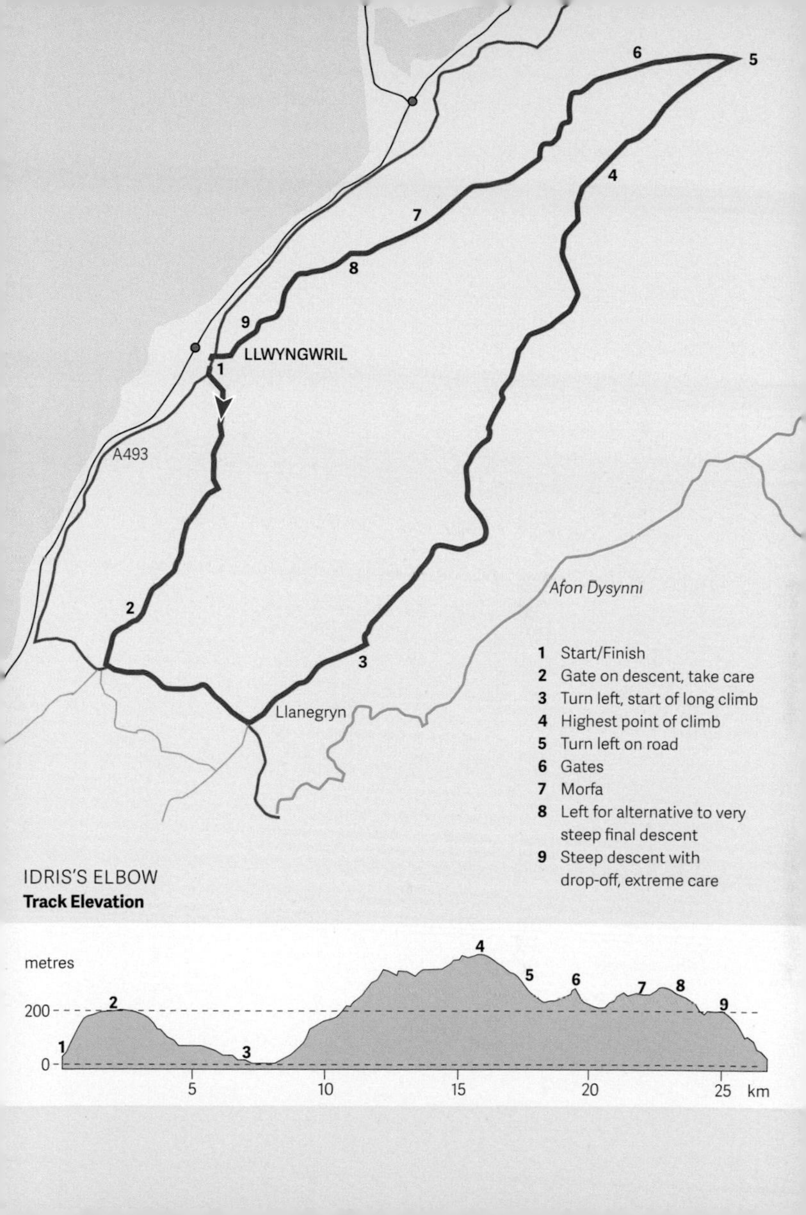
6
5
4
7
8
9
LLWYNGWRIL
1
A493
Afon Dysynni
2
3
Llanegryn
1 Start/Finish
2 Gate on descent, take care
3 Turn left, start of long climb
4 Highest point of climb
5 Turn left on road
6 Gates
7 Morfa
8 Left for alternative to very steep final descent
9 Steep descent with drop-off, extreme care
IDRIS'S ELBOW
Track Elevation
metres
200
0
5
10
15
20
25
km

too technical, although there is a tricky right-hand bend near some rock outcrops.

The gradient eases just before you reach a road; turn left onto it. This then climbs steeply uphill, over the rock outcrops, then goes steeply down. There are more gates on this section to slow you down, but they provide opportunities to enjoy the scenery without concentrating on preventing your wheels running into ruts and potholes.

The road (its official classification, but it's a farm track really) climbs through the conifer plantation you passed earlier, then undulates south-west across an open area called Morfa, Morfa being the old Welsh word for marshland.

This leads to the final descent into Llwyngwril. There are some wonderful views of Barmouth Bay on this section, but pay attention as the track gets steeper. Keep left where another trail goes off right, although that is a good road alternative back to Llwyngwril if the next section bothers you.

This descends very steeply, and there is an even steeper drop-off just to the right of the trail. Walk down if you aren't comfortable with it. Eventually you reach a walled track that leads back to Llwyngwril.

17 Snowdon by Bike

A ride up and down Britain's second-highest mountain

DIFFICULTY RATING **10/10** WILDNESS RATING **8/10**

This is hard but rewarding. The best cycle route up and down Snowdon is the Llanberis Path. It shadows the incredible rack-and-pinion Snowdon Mountain Railway (built 1894 to 1896), and the path is very steep and rough in places. You have to dismount occasionally and push your bike, or even carry it, both going up and coming down.

This is a ride for the fit, and possibly best done on a mountain bike with a good range of gears. A cyclo-cross bike would be OK, so long as it has low enough gears. You gain almost 1,000 metres in height in just 7 kilometres of riding, an average gradient of just under 14%. That's tough.

FACT FILE

Where Snowdon is in North Wales, 13 kilometres south-east of Caernarfon

OS grid ref SH 5829 5962

Start/Finish Llanberis on the A4086

Ride distance 14 kilometres (8.75 miles)

Highest point Snowdon summit (1,085 metres)

Approximate time 3.5 to 4-plus hours

Llanberis Path starts as a continuation of Victoria Terrace, the last road on your right going south-east out of Llanberis on the A4086. The terrace quickly becomes a narrow lane, where the gradient is already relentless. After passing a few isolated buildings you turn left off the road that follows Llanberis Path. This is a proper trail; rough in places, better in others, all the way to the top.

You soon reach a section of rough-cut steps; there will be more, as well as other rocky, un-rideable sections. Remembering the locations of these going up will make your descent safer: you will need to dismount at some of them going down. Thankfully, though, there are long rideable sections both ways.

Around halfway the path follows the railway more closely, and you might see one of the diesel or steam locomotives and its single carriage click-clacking its way to the summit. Halfway House, a café in one of the wildest places, is good for a brew and something sustaining. Then it's onwards and upwards. The path

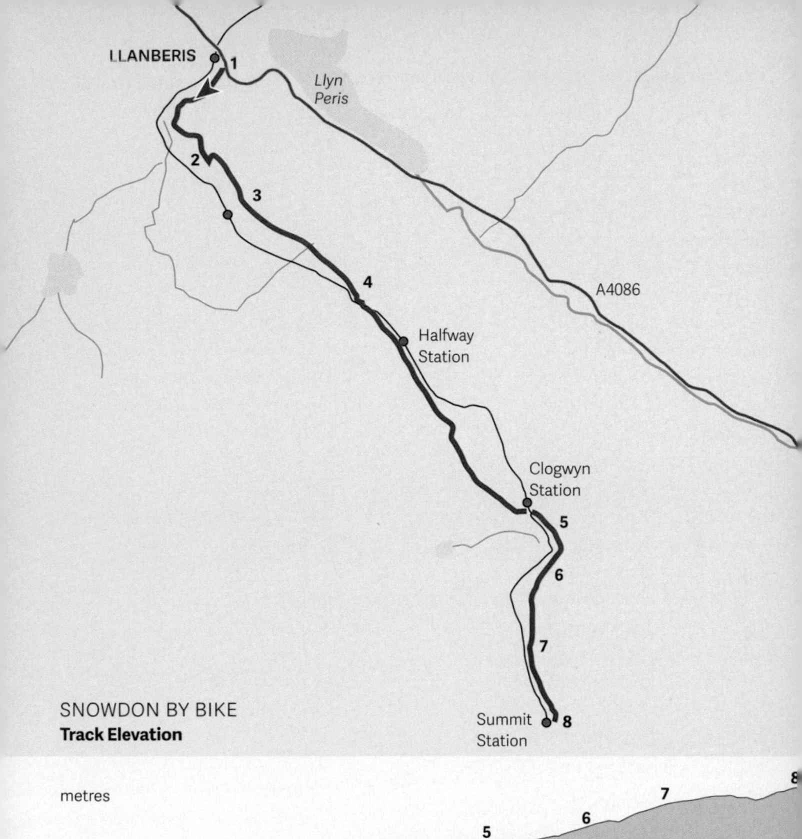

SNOWDON BY BIKE
Track Elevation

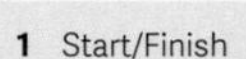

1 Start/Finish
2 Turn left off metalled road to follow Llanberis Path
3 Steep section with steps
4 Very long steep section
5 Exposed, stay away from the edge
6 Very steep
7 Exposed, especially on east side, where embankment has been built for safety
8 Hafod Erui, Snowdon Visitor Centre, hot drinks and cake

narrows slightly at first, and it's rough, but not for long.

You next meet the railway after a very steep pull to Clogwyn Station, where you go under the line and need a good head for heights for what's on the other side. Some find the exposure here a bit daunting, because the mountainside drops for several hundred metres over an arc of crags. It's quite safe. Just keep away from the edge.

The exposure doesn't last long, but there's more of it a kilometre later near the summit. It's hard to get there, but the feeling of achievement and the views when you do are immense. Enjoy the summit, then take care on the descent so you can enjoy that too.

The best cycle route up and down Snowdon is the Llanberis Path. It shadows the incredible rack-and-pinion Snowdon Mountain Railway, and the path is very steep and rough in places.

Finally, a word about when to do this ride. Llanberis Path gets busy at weekends and during holiday periods, so it's best mid-week in spring or autumn. Check the weather before you set off, and don't attempt this ride if the forecast is bad. It's serious mountain stuff.

18 Clwyddian Clogger

A mix of little lanes, trails and a main road pass in the Clwyddian Range of North Wales

DIFFICULTY RATING **8/10** WILDNESS RATING **7/10**

I was introduced to the Clwyddian Range by a Liverpool cyclist called Duff Fawcett. He's a lifelong rider brought up in the old ways of adventurous club rides, when even racing cyclists didn't so much train as use their bikes to explore, and got fit in the process. Fawcett was a good racer, but he's gone back to his roots now, and he rides for the pure pleasure and adventure of doing it.

'I've always loved looking at maps, and I still do. I'm always wondering, what's that road like? Or I see a road while I'm out on another ride and wonder, where does that go? My wife Hannah is the same – she grew up in a family of explorers. We like to find tracks, then explore them, which is how this ride came about,' he said.

I've not replicated Duff's ride, because there was a lot more road in it, but I've stuck to its wild heart for this jaunt around the voluptuous folds of the Clwyddian Range, a chain of hills that runs north-west to south-east from Prestatyn to just south of Ruthin, where the ride starts. The range is full of wild cycling opportunities – some challenging, others less so. Cyclo-cross or gravel bikes are best for this one; a mountain bike would be OK too.

Head out from the town centre, south-east past the hospital, and keep right to the B5429, where you turn right. Follow this road south to a 90-degree right bend, and turn left. You then flick quickly right and left, past a few houses, to start the first long climb, which Fawcett calls 'Shelf', and it's epic.

Over the first 1.3 kilometres a reasonable road surface breaks down into farm track, while the gradient is unrelenting. It's a fantastic scenic slog up to the crux of the climb, an

FACT FILE

Where Ruthin is 17 miles north-west of Wrexham and 8 miles south-east of Denbigh

OS grid ref SJ 5912 0953

Start/Finish Eastern edge of Ruthin town centre

Ride distance 25 kilometres (15.6 miles)

Highest points Top of the Shelf (359 metres), top of Penbarras Pass (361 metres)

Approximate time 2–3 hours

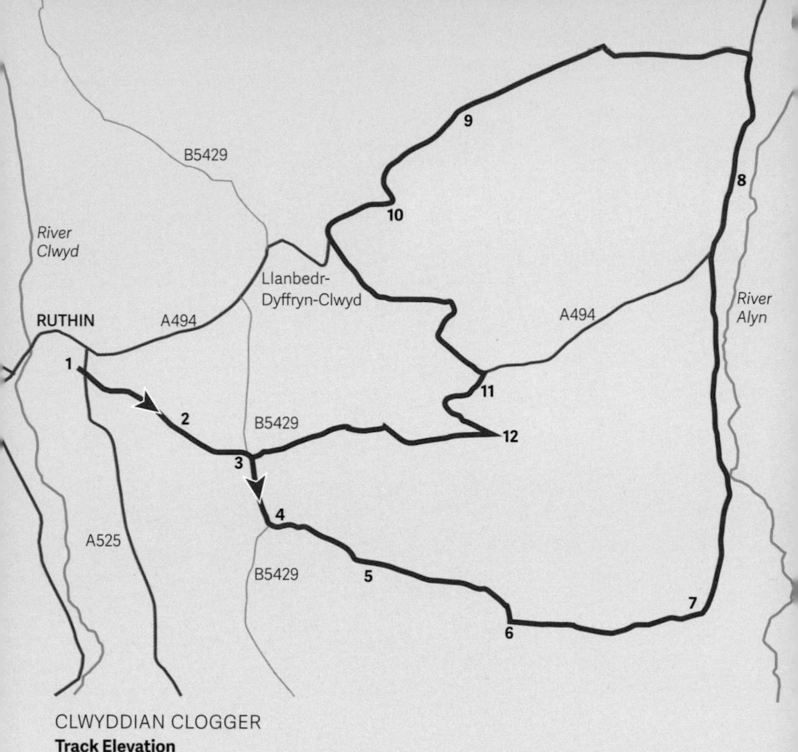

CLWYDDIAN CLOGGER

Track Elevation

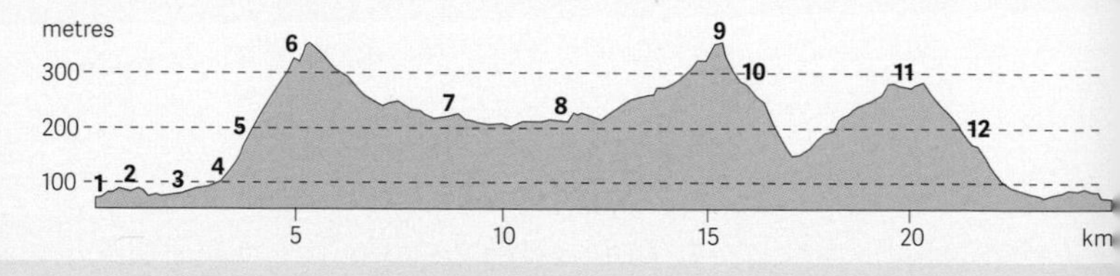

1 Start/Finish
2 Out and back on same road
3 Turn right and head south
4 Go left at right bend
5 Start of very steep 3 kilometres uphill
6 The hairpin
7 Go left and head north
8 Two kilometres of main road
9 Top of Penbarras Pass
10 Steep descent and cattle grids
11 Right onto trail at top of main road
12 Badly rutted hairpin

unfeasibly steep hairpin bend after two kilometres of 13% climbing. By now the hard-packed stone track has deteriorated to loose gravel, so pedalling around the hairpin bend requires strength and impeccable technique.

The hairpin has a 25% gradient at least. The key to riding up it is to take the inside line, the steepest bit of the bend, because the surface on the outside is too loose to keep traction. When I first experienced it with Fawcett's cycling club, Liverpool Braveheart, a good few young, fit riders who had climbed ahead of the rest lower down didn't make it through the hairpin.

Indeed, nobody did, until an old hand, Simon Locke, hit the inside, held on and powered round. Fawcett made it too, with son Sean just ahead of him. Hannah Fawcett walked, choosing dignity over the macho death struggle her men were engaged in. But Alison Howell made it round, smiling all the way, with a crowd of clubmates having stopped by now to encourage everybody up. It is fun to try – even those who fell off that day got up smiling. However, walking around the hairpin is safer, easier, and far more dignified.

A short, final, but still steep straight section leads to the summit at 359 metres, where trail becomes road for the fast descent – take care – to Llanarmon-yn-Lal. Turn first left in the village, and head north along the River Alyn valley. Eventually you reach the A494: go right, and continue north for two more kilometres, then go first left after Llanferres village.

A little lane joins the Penbarras Pass, where you go left and continue to the top of the pass. Moel Famau, the highest peak in the Clwyddian Range at 554 metres, is 2 kilometres north of here. There are lots of mountain-bike trails in Moel Famau Country Park.

Cross the cattle grid to start the very steep descent. After just under a kilometre there is a sharp right hairpin that demands respect. There's another cattle grid shortly after that: take great care, especially in wet conditions. Walking around cattle grids, where possible, is sometimes a safer option.

You eventually reach the A494 in Llanbedr-Dyffryn-Clwyd. Turn left, climb to the summit of the A494 pass, called locally 'the Bwlch', which can be busy with traffic, and at the summit look for the entrance to a bridleway on your right. Take great care turning right onto the bridleway.

Follow the bridleway, ignoring a track that goes left at a right bend, because it's a footpath, and continue down through a conifer plantation, where there is a very tight right-hand hairpin. Take care there, because the trail is very chewed up and broken. After that, it's straight down to the B5429. Go right, then first left, Maes-y-Llan Road, then cross the Vale of Clwyd to return to Ruthin.

6

The Midlands

19 Cotswold Canter

Follow old roads and bridleways across the fields and down seductive valleys in chocolate-box countryside

DIFFICULTY RATING **8/10** WILDNESS RATING **8/10**

The Cotswold Hills are poetry in landscape: a rolling patchwork of open fields and woods, with villages the colour of cinder toffee and glass-clear rivers. Laid across this landscape is a lattice of little lanes, old Roman roads and bridleways. It's horse country, so you will probably meet a few on this ride, but we can all share if we consider each other's space.

The ride starts in tourist-trapping Stow-on-the-Wold, where antique emporia and cute cafés abound. The buildings are made from Cotswold stone, a fossil-rich limestone quarried locally that varies in colour depending on which part of the Cotswolds it originates from. It's warmest, most cinder toffee, here in the central Cotswolds.

From Market Square head south-west down Church Street; go right on Sheep Street, then do a right and immediate left across the busy A429. Head for Lower Swell, keeping right at the grass triangle in the village centre, and follow this road to its crossroads with Condicote Lane, and turn right.

This is part of Ryknild Street, a Roman Road that ran from this area up to South Yorkshire, and was an offshoot of the more famous Exeter-to-Lincoln Fosse Way. The surface of Condicote Lane is OK at first, but it gets rougher before crossing the B4077, and deteriorates a lot straight after it. Tough going, but the tough going doesn't last long, and the trail improves nearer Condicote. Keep left at the church, and go left again where this road forks.

Turn right at the next T-junction, then almost immediatey left onto a bridleway that goes through some trees. Follow it out of the trees, then go right where the bridleway forks. Now, the left trail is tempting – it

FACT FILE

Where 20 kilometres east of Cheltenham

OS grid ref SP 1914 2580

Start/Finish Market Place, Stow-on-the-Wold

Ride distance 40 kilometres (25 miles)

Highest point Cutsdean Hill (293 metres)

Approximate time 4–5 hours.

would be easier to ride on – but you can't, because it's a footpath. The right trail, the bridleway, goes across a field, and it is heavy going, but stick with it, because after a kilometre it becomes a good road.

Go straight over the next crossroads, through Cutsdean, then left at the crossroads. Cross the B4077 again, going south now. Turn right just after the left turn to Temple Guiting, climb the steep hill and descend into a wood. The next section is gorgeous, especially in spring when the leaves are fresh. Take the next left to climb out of the wood, then go left to Guiting Power. Cross the River Windrush and go immediately left to Barton, along the Windrush valley.

The Windrush is a lovely little river, unremarkable in itself, yet it gave its name to a ship, then a generation. The British Nationality Act was passed in 1948, offering British citizenship to residents of the Commonwealth provided they came to live in the UK. The ship, *Empire Windrush*, was in passenger service after the Second World War, and in 1948 it docked in Kingston, Jamaica, en route to Britain, but it was far from full.

So the owners offered cheap passage to anyone who wanted it, and 492 people took up their offer. They sailed

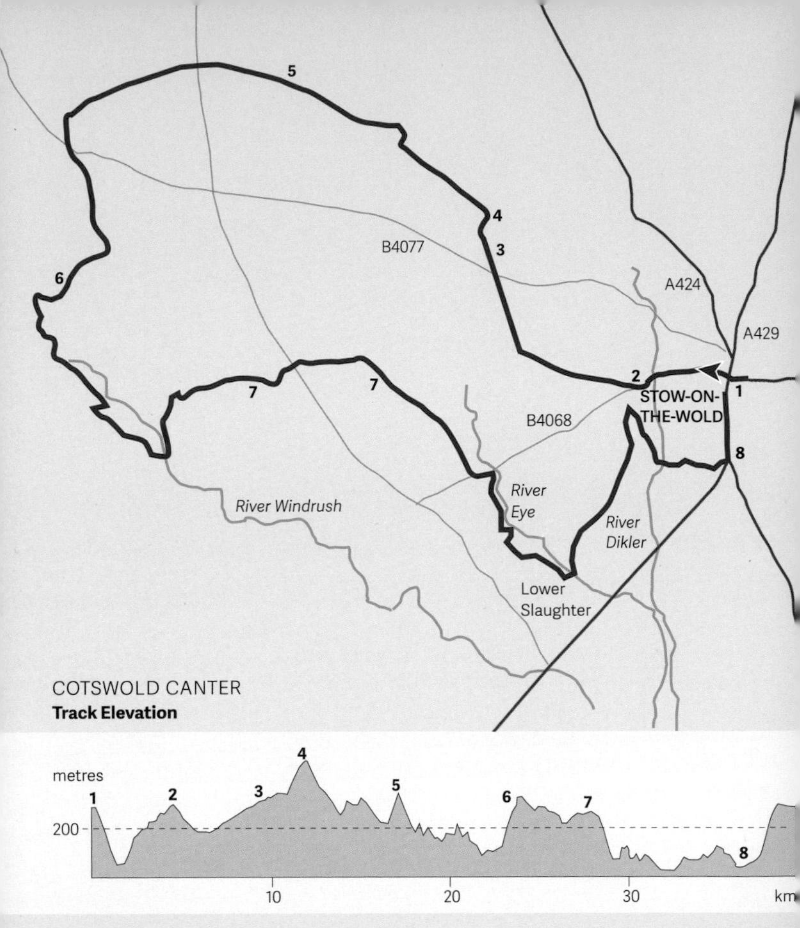

1 Start/Finish
2 Keep right
3 Trail deteriorates
4 Left at church
5 Heavy going
6 Steep climb followed by steep descent
7 Long bridleway section
8 Take care on main road

This very picturesque place is one of the 52 'Thankful Villages' of England: villages that lost no men during the First World War.

to England and, applying their right under the Nationality Act, started new lives here, the first of many Caribbeans to do so. The original 492 are known now as the Windrush Generation.

Turn right in Barton to join a trail, then keep left. Go left on the first road, and continue straight at the next crossroads, past some quarries on Chalk Hill. Once you reach a small copse there's a trail on your right. Head down it and into Eyford Park. The trail runs through the gardens of this Baroque-style stately home, and at one point it's right next to the driveway, so you can indulge some illusions of grandeur. Well, for a few hundred metres, at least.

Eventually you reach the B4068: turn left after 400 metres, just before the bridge over the River Eye, and go right onto a bridleway that leads through some woods and follows the river to Upper Slaughter.

This very picturesque place is one of the 52 'Thankful Villages' of England: villages that lost no men during the First World War. It looks thankful, too, and if anything Lower Slaughter is even more attractive. Turn right when you get to the road in Upper Slaughter, go right again, then take the second left. Head south across the crossroads and go left to make a splendid entrance into Lower Slaughter alongside the River Eye.

Cross the river and head north-east to Lower Swell, but turn right onto Mill Lane as you approach the first buildings. The lane quickly changes to bridleway; cross the River Dikler, and go left where the trail joins a road. Turn left on the A429 for the last kilometre back to Stow-on-the-Wold.

20 Malvern Hills
A ridge ride in the Midlands along an outlier of the Welsh mountains

DIFFICULTY RATING **6/10** WILDNESS RATING **7/10**

The Malvern Hills are beautiful seen from any direction, but their siren call is particularly strong amid the madness of the M5. That's how I saw them so many times on so many journeys, each time promising myself I'd turn off and explore them one day. When I did I wasn't disappointed.

The Malvern Hills are wilderness in the Midlands, outliers of Welsh mountains, beloved by artists, writers, poets and composers. They were Elgar's muse, and the inspiration for *Piers Plowman*. They are an absolute glory to explore by bike, as the keen cyclist Edward Elgar did many times.

Following a ridge, hill top by hill top, is a sublime experience, and the Malverns provide it in accessible form. North to south the hills stand like a regiment, a stubborn chain of 680-million-year-old rock. Wales is west of them, while the Severn Valley and the rolling fields of the Midlands lie east. Geography here is simple, so precisely aligned.

You could start from any car park around the hills, so long as the way out of it is a bridleway. I chose North Quarry because I like the logic of going north to south, but it's a brutal start with a terrific view – eventually. A deep-breathing, silent, out-of-the-saddle haul, interspersed by grim footslogging, leads almost to the top of North Hill, where everything the map promises rolls out before you. Long and rideable, the trail is slung like hammocks between a series of peaks.

Visit the summit of North Hill if you wish, then set forth south to Worcestershire Beacon. Ten of the 21 Malvern Hills break the 1,000-foot barrier; most lie on the north-south axis, and they nearly all have bridleways to their summits. At 435 metres, though, Worcestershire

FACT FILE

Where Great Malvern is in Worcestershire, 12 kilometres west of junction 7 of the M5

OS grid ref SO 7697 4694

Start/Finish North Quarry car park

Ride distance 22 kilometres (13.75 miles)

Highest point Worcestershire Beacon (435 metres)

Approximate time 3–4 hours

7
1
2
West
Malvern
3
6
Lower
Wyche
Upper
Colwall
4
B4218
A449
5
Little
Malvern
1 North Quarry car park
2 Very hard first section
3 Exposed summit
4 Take care crossing road, very steep start to next off-road section
5 Steep downhill, walking recommended
6 Short off-road section
MALVERN HILLS
Track Elevation
metres
300
200
5
10
15
km

Beacon is the highest, and just about the most improbable place to find a café. It's not there now, though: surprisingly, the Beacon Café didn't blow away, but was burned to the ground in 1989. Building another has, weirdly, been banned by parliament.

The view from Worcestershire Beacon is breathtaking, and there's a toposcope on the summit to identify exactly what you can see. It's the land of hope and glory that inspired Elgar, and this exact spot had the 14th-century poet William Langland pen one of the oldest classics of English literature. It's called *Piers Plowman*, and begins, 'On a May Morning on a Malvern hillside, as I lay and leaned and looked on the water, I slumbered and slept, so sweetly it murmured.'

Water made Great Malvern, as well as all the villages fanning out from it that cling like a collar to the line of springs around the hills. Water was bottled and sold here long before Jacob Schweppes set up in 1850. Sixty springs circle the hills, and water flows from them at a steady 8.3 degrees Celsius. The water is filtered rain, so very pure, a valuable commodity back in the days when water was generally so dirty that most people drank beer.

In Elgar's time, when Great Malvern was a thriving spa, the water filled open pools where people bathed. Water cures were big business, freely prescribed for mental as well as physical problems. Alfred, Lord

The view from Worcestershire Beacon is breathtaking, and there's a toposcope on the summit to identify exactly what you can see.

Tennyson, was treated in Malvern after a nervous breakdown; so was Charles Darwin's sister. To help her, Charles underwent the same treatment, which involved cold baths, drinking lots of water, eating fruit and going for long walks in the hills; an 18th-century detox for body and soul.

You pass the Morris Well in Wyche after riding off Worcestershire Beacon. Be careful: the trail from the summit is steep and slippery; it's safer to walk until the gradient relents. Anything with a name that looks or sounds like 'wich', as in Wyche or Droitwich, denotes a connection with salt. The road running through this natural cutting in the hills was an old salt road through the Malverns into Wales.

The next climb leads to the top of Jubilee Hill. You can see the county boundary between Worcestershire and Herefordshire here because it traces a long earthwork called the Shire Ditch. It runs all along the spine of the southern Malvern Hills. The ditch wasn't built to keep people in or out: it was built 700 years ago by the Earl of Gloucester to stop his deer straying onto the lands of the Bishop of Hereford.

The bridleway off Jubilee Hill follows a double hairpin down to Malvern Wells, and the last section is very steep and often wet because it's under trees, so walking is recommended again. Sorry, there's quite a bit of walking on this ride.

Turn right at the junction where the bridleway joins a metalled road, then right again onto the A449, which you follow for a kilometre to a gap in the hills. Go right on the B4232 just after the gap. This road runs along the western edge of the Malverns; it has glorious views and goes through some lovely quiet villages. Follow it north, taking in a short section of bridleway on your right through the Summer Hill car park, then re-join the B4232 and continue north to West Malvern. You turn left here down a steep hill, then turn right where you see the sign for the Worcestershire Way.

This section of what is a long-distance footpath runs from West Malvern along bridleways and some tiny lanes to Ankerdine Hill, a celebrated hill climb in local cycling circles. But to complete this ride you turn off the Worcestershire Way well short of Ankerdine by taking the second bridleway on your right. All that's left is to climb a very steep hill through some lovely woodland, then turn left on the B4232 and follow that road back to North Quarry car park. The Malverns are yours forever now; visit again soon.

21 Wild Brum

A canal towpath ride in the middle of a huge bustling city

DIFFICULTY RATING **2/10** WILDNESS RATING **5/10**

There are said to be more canals in Birmingham than in Venice, and they certainly add a different dimension to Britain's second-biggest city. Canals have a special charm, and even though they were built to serve the early years of the Industrial Revolution they are wild places now.

We start in the heart of the city at the Gas Street Basin. It's a stone's throw from city-centre landmarks like the Mailbox, but the basin is another world in plain sight where people live gently on the water next to buzzing office blocks. The basin even has its own pub and café.

Canals radiate in all directions. They link with major rivers like the Trent, Severn and the Thames. They also link cities – this ride explores the Birmingham Mainline Canal, but I reckon it's possible to ride alongside canals from Birmingham all the way to Manchester. I might try it one day. This web of water is why Birmingham became such an important place during the Industrial Revolution. Canals carried raw materials to the factories, and exported finished products out to our cities and ports.

Of course, it's not the canals you ride, but their towpaths. Towpaths form a flat boundary along most of the canal network. They were made for horses to pull the barges before diesel engines took over the job. Towpaths vary from surfaced cycleways, through hard earth trails to well-maintained grassy strips, so towpath-riding suits almost any bike fitted with substantial tyres. You will always find some towpaths not so well maintained, but none on this ride.

One word of caution about towpath cycling: you're supposed to get a permit to ride them. It isn't a drama, because you download permits from this link, and fill in the details yourself: http://www.waterscape.com/

FACT FILE

Where Central Birmingham

OS grid ref SP 0600 8690

Start/Finish Gas Street Basin

Ride distance 16 kilometres (10 miles)

Highest point The bridges

Approximate time 1–2 hours

YEOFORD
Nº
B'HAM CANAL BOAT SERVICES LTD
ASH

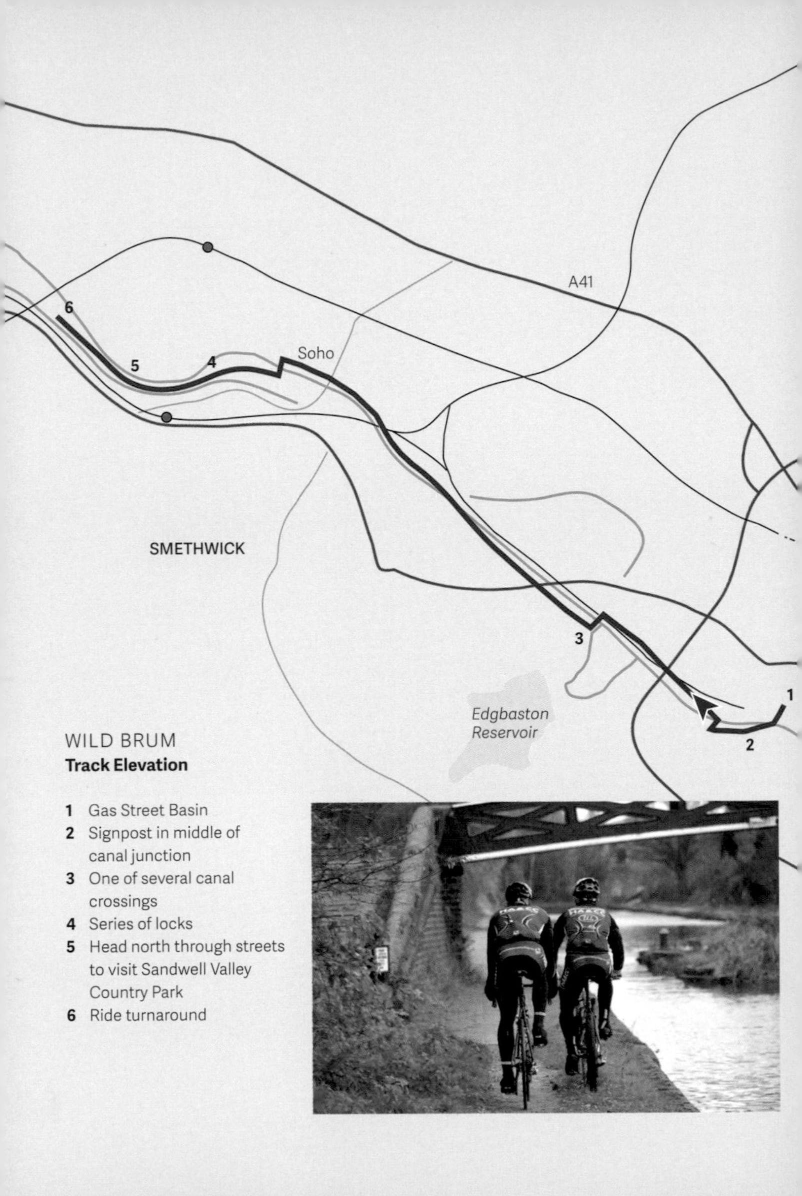

A41
Soho
SMETHWICK
Edgbaston Reservoir
1
2
3
4
5
6
WILD BRUM
Track Elevation
1 Gas Street Basin
2 Signpost in middle of canal junction
3 One of several canal crossings
4 Series of locks
5 Head north through streets to visit Sandwell Valley Country Park
6 Ride turnaround

things-to-do/cycling/permit. There's a code of conduct too, which cyclists must abide by, but the rules are simple: just good manners. Don't forget to take the permit with you.

Within 100 metres of setting off you come to the first canal junction. Like road junctions, directions are on signposts; the signpost here is on an island with ducks and swans swimming around its base. The National Sea Life Centre is on the other side of this liquid roundabout.

You'd think riding along a canal would be flat, but it's not entirely. Every offshoot canal, and there are plenty near the city centre, means a bridge with a steep incline over it and down the other side. The bridges are often cobbled, too, so horses' hooves could get some grip.

There are similar ups and downs where the canal is crossed by a bridge and the towpath doesn't go under it. This happened a lot when the first canals were built, because it was another level of engineering to build bridges wide enough to incorporate the canal and the towpath.

The old boatmen were pretty nifty on their feet, because as they approached pathless bridges they jumped off their barges, untied the horse, and led it over the top of the bridge while the barge continued under its own momentum. Then they linked the horse up with the barge again on the other side.

Bargemen and women worked even harder when they reached a tunnel. Momentum isn't enough to take a barge through a long tunnel, so bargemen and women laid on their backs on top of the barge and powered it through by walking along the tunnel walls. The process was called 'legging it', and it's where the slang expression to 'leg it' comes from. It was strenuous work and required good technique. Professional 'leggers' were available at long tunnels, and compulsory for the longest ones, like Stannage, which goes under the Pennines from Yorkshire to Lancashire. Full-time professional 'leggers' were by nature formidable athletes.

Riding canal towpaths is relaxing, but there's also something illicit, sneaky, even, about riding the urban towpaths. You see the town or city's other face, the one not made up for public viewing – its backyard – and can you learn a lot by rummaging through backyards. There are different people to meet too: people who live on barges, or regular towpath walkers, and they are both parts of an alternative city.

So take as long as you like on this one, and ride as far as you want. We've supplied a map, and you can turn around and ride back to Gas Street Basin exactly where it indicates. Having said that, the turnaround is just south of another wild Birmingham, Sandwell Valley Country Park, so you could explore the cycle trails there. And of course you could just carry on.

22 Robin Hood Rides Again

Explore the forest home of a folk legend, the stately home of a real-life duke, and a truly delightful river

DIFFICULTY RATING **6/10** WILDNESS RATING **7/10**

There's been a forest here since the end of the Ice Age; core samples containing ancient tree pollen prove that. Forests intrigue people; they are mysterious by nature – sometimes dark, sometimes dense – but even an open forest has no horizon, so you just don't know who or what could be lurking in them. It makes forests the perfect place to hide.

That facet of Sherwood Forest, more than any historical fact, gave rise to the legend of Robin Hood. Sherwood was his playground while he robbed the rich, then bolted back to the green wood to spread largesse among the poor. It was wealth redistribution, 12th-century style. And Robin Hood still contributes to the wealth of the local community, through tourism. It's a role far friendlier than pointing a sharp piece of steel at somebody's throat and growling, 'Giz yer money' in his victim's ear.

The forest is much smaller now; it occupies a thin strip of land 20 miles long and at the most 5 miles wide, and stretches from just north of Nottingham to Worksop. But back in the days when Robin was robbing, the forest spilled westwards into Derbyshire and north into South Yorkshire. And much of today's Sherwood is relatively new, although some of the original forest still exists. If only the 800-year-old Major Oak could talk, it might confirm if the Robin Hood legend was true.

This ride starts at the Sherwood Forest visitor centre near Edwinstowe, and for the first section you head north, following signs to the Major Oak. It is remarkable to see a living thing so old: there's a wonderful peace about it, and a tangible presence. That peace lingers as you continue north-

FACT FILE

Where Nottinghamshire, Sherwood Forest and the Dukeries are 10 miles east of Chesterfield and 18 miles west of Lincoln

OS grid ref SK 626 677

Start/Finish Sherwood Forest Visitor Centre

Ride distance 23 kilometres (14.4 miles)

Highest point Between the start and the Major Oak (80 metres)

Approximate time 2–3 hours

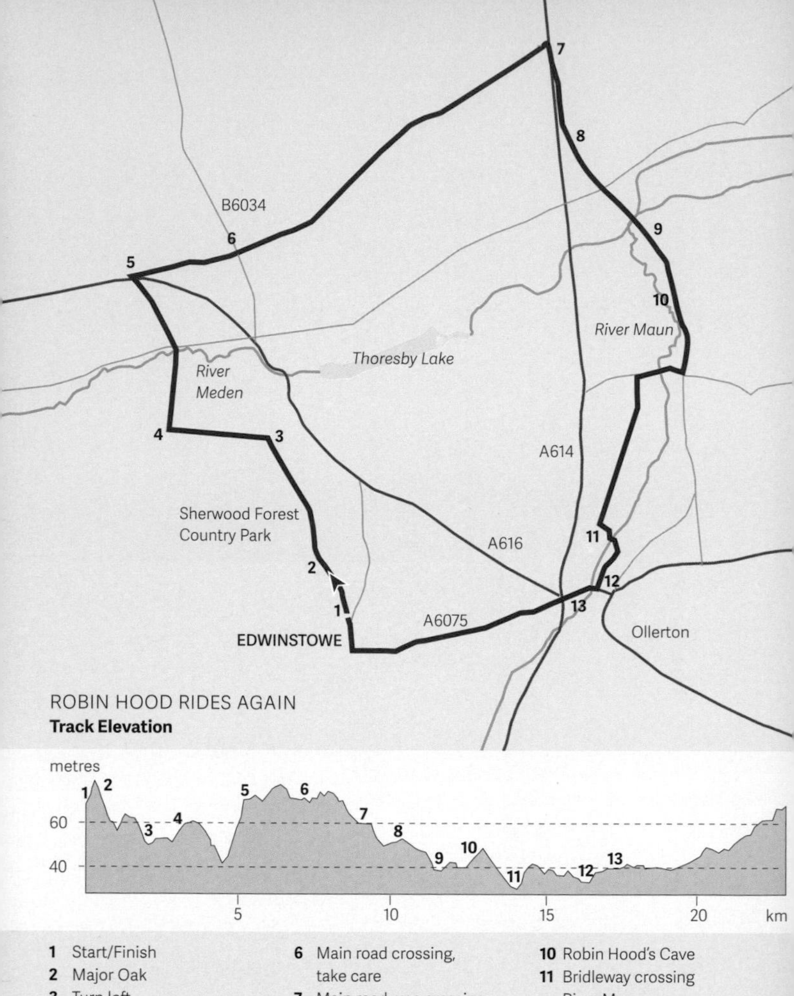

1 Start/Finish
2 Major Oak
3 Turn left
4 Turn right
5 Follow trail going east out of car park
6 Main road crossing, take care
7 Main road, use crossing
8 Follow trail, can be overgrown
9 Sometimes wet and muddy here
10 Robin Hood's Cave
11 Bridleway crossing River Maun
12 Turn right
13 Very busy roundabout, take care

west through an area of the forest called Birklands. This is the site of the Thyngow, an ancient gathering place that acted as an early court, settling disputes over land and resolving broken promises.

Carry on north-west, and you leave the forest to cross an area of heathland leading to a five-way trail junction. Turn left, then take the next trail right, crossing Netherfield Lane then the much bigger A616, to Hazel Gap car park. The trail you've just followed continues east along the southern edge of Gibraltar Plantation, forming an acute angle to the A616. Follow this trail, cross the B6034, and you are in Clumber Park.

The park was created by über-gardener Capability Brown for the Dukes of Newcastle. There are loads of opportunities for off-the-beaten-track cycling in Clumber, which is owned now by the National Trust. It's a great habitat for wildlife, with rare birds like the nightjar, woodlark, redstart and water rail thriving in Clumber.

The countryside around Clumber is an appealingly soft and gently rolling landscape, and it caught the eyes of more dukes than the Newcastles. There are four contiguous ducal estates in North Nottinghamshire, with the Duke of Portland's Welbeck right next to Clumber. The four estates are why this area is sometimes called the Dukeries.

There are a few road crossings on

this ride, but the next, across the busy A614, has a pelican crossing to help you onto the Robin Hood Way, going south. The first section was rough and overgrown when I rode it, but I got through, with patience and a few dismounts. You eventually cross the rivers Maun and Meden, which join at the bridge but are separated again a few metres further downstream by a weir. They eventually join fully and become the River Idle.

Continue south, but take care, because the next section can be very muddy and slippery. Sometimes there's so much standing water on either side of the trail here that some trees have died, creating at times a prehistoric swamp look. We are right above the Dukeries coalfield here, and in places it looks as though coal is being formed today.

But keep following the trail and conditions soon dry out. About a

kilometre after the muddy section you cross a large outcrop of dry red sandstone beside the River Maun. The Maun is called Whitewater for this particular stretch, because it flows through a long wriggle of tight bends, which creates turbulence when the river is full. It's not Lava Falls on the Colorado River, but it's enough to give a gentle British water course a short feisty feel.

There's a place on the river here marked on the map as Robin Hood's Cave. Sounds romantic, and you have to stand on a little cliff above the water's edge to see it, but it doesn't look like a robber's refuge to me. I suppose it could have been created during a flood, but it looks more like someone hollowed out a bit of the cliff face.

Continuing south, you reach a road; turn right, cross the bridge and take the first left. Follow this trail past Whitewater Farm, over another bridge, and into New Ollerton. Turn right onto the A6075, and follow signs back to Edwinstowe and the Sherwood Forest Visitor Centre to complete this ride.

The Dukeries tend to get overlooked in pursuit of more exotic cycling destinations nearby, like the Peak District, which is a shame. It's a lovely place for cycling, with lots of quiet lanes and bridleways to explore. The gentle meandering rivers here are lovely too. Give this ride a try and you'll soon see why those posh old dukes built their houses here.

23 The Leicestershire Stakes

A mix of trails inspired by a modern bike race and a much older form of sport, set in rural Leicestershire

DIFFICULTY RATING **6/10** WILDNESS RATING **6/10**

This ride explores an area made famous in cycling by the Melton CiCLE Classic, a major British road race that pursues a wild-cycling ethic by mixing narrow lanes with rough bridleways. The route is also redolent of the landscape that gave steeplechasing to horse racing, and created the first off-road sport for cyclists, which is still going strong.

Burrough Hill Country Park's car park is the best place to start. Turn right and head for the honey-stone village of Somerby, the Parachute Regiment's former training base for the Second World War raid on Arnhem. Take the third right, Manor Lane.

This soon becomes a bridleway. Look dead ahead where it starts and you'll see the next village, Owston, and its church steeple. Somerby's church steeple is behind you, and the bridleway links the two. Terrain like this gave horse racing the steeplechase, where the original steeplechase jockeys rode around big circuits of open country using church steeples to navigate. They covered the terrain by the straightest route they could, jumping hedges and gates, which were eventually represented on racecourses as fences.

The first cyclo-cross races, which were held in France at the start of the 20th century, were run off on this steeplechase basis. Competitors did one big lap of towns and villages, using church steeples to find their way.

Follow the bridleway to Owston, which gets indistinct in places, but if you are in doubt it hugs the hedgerows, so use them to find the trail. It joins a road just outside Owston: follow it almost into the village, but turn right before you enter. Then, when you get to a sharp left bend in the road, look right, and take the trail that leads away from it. This descends at first, then after crossing

FACT FILE

Where Five kilometres due south of Melton Mowbray in Leicestershire

OS grid ref SK 7650 1152

Start/Finish Burrough Hill Country Park

Ride distance 31 kilometres (19.4 miles)

Highest point Tilton on the Hill (212 metres)

Approximate time 3–4 hours

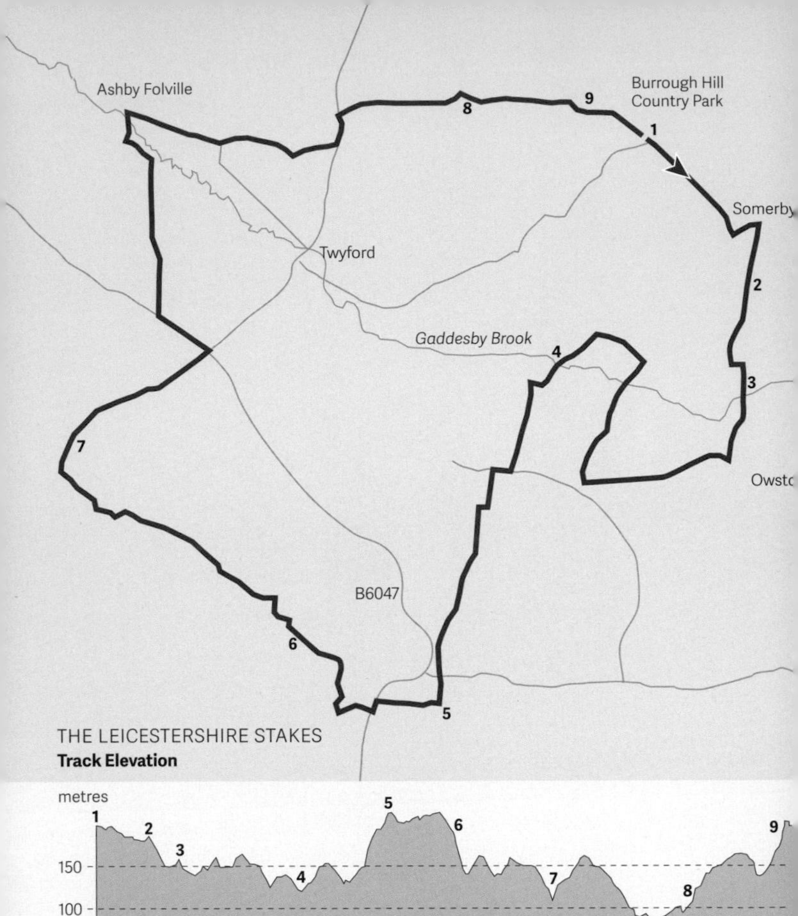

THE LEICESTERSHIRE STAKES

Track Elevation

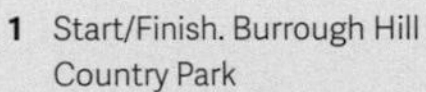

1 Start/Finish. Burrough Hill Country Park
2 First off-road section
3 Trail indistinct, look for it near hedges
4 Careful crossing stream
5 Highest point of the ride, great views south
6 Steep descent
7 Trail indistinct in places
8 Steep uphill
9 Iron Age fort

a stream there's a short drag up to Newbold.

Turn left in Newbold and go 500 metres along Newbold Road, then take the bridleway on your left. Pass Newbold Grange Farm and keep following the bridleway, taking care at the stream under the trees, to White House Farm. Go left on Dawson's Lane, then turn right at the T-junction, then left on a trail called Blackspinney Lane. This passes through a gap in an old railway embankment, and meets a road just before Tilton on the Hill.

Continue south on this road, through the village, past the church, and turn right on Back Lane. Continue west on this road until it meets the B6047, where you go left, then first right, and look on your right for a sign indicating the Midshires Way.

The Midshires Way is a boon to cyclists across a wide area. It's a 230-mile footpath classified as bridleway for much of its distance. It runs from the Chilterns through the Midlands to Stockport near Manchester, linking the Ridgeway in the south with the Trans-Pennine Trail in the north. In doing so it presents huge opportunities for wild cycling.

The first section of trail is rutted in places, but that is followed by a long downhill sweep to Hammer's Lodge Farm. Follow the trail through the farm, and over Queniborough Brook. You hit a road next; go right, then first left onto a bridleway. The next section tests navigation skills, because the trail is indistinct in places. Basically, head on a north-west bearing. White's Barn is the only building you can see, so head towards it.

Carry on past White's Barn to Hartfield Lodge, then go right. The farming landscape here owes much to the wool boom of the 1700s, when arable fields that supported villages were turned to grassland for sheep. Lots of villages were lost; all that's left of them today are ridges that marked their fields. You bump over quite a few of them during this part of the ride.

Go left on the next road, then take the trail right at Freezeland Lodge. This is a long off-road section, but the trail is mostly straight and easy to follow. The bit after crossing Gaddesby Brook ends at a road just east of Ashby Folville, a village named after the flight here in the 1300s by inhabitants of a French town called Folleville. Not all the newcomers improved the neighbourhood.

Eustace Folville and two of his brothers, one of whom was a priest, formed a gang of robbers. Their criminal career began in 1326, when they ambushed and murdered Sir Roger Bellere in Charnwood Forest. Bellere had 50 soldiers with him, so the Folville gang was a bit tasty.

They disappeared for a while after that, but two years later the Folvilles were ripping round Leicestershire and neighbouring counties, robbing the rich and keeping the loot for themselves. By 1330 Eustace Folville was wanted for three robberies, four murders and a rape. Rape didn't mean what it does today: it described any physical offence from assault to abduction.

Eventually Eustace got too much for King Edward II, who said he'd pardon him if he fought on the English side against the Scots. It was a deal, and Eustace became a very successful soldier, eventually retiring with honour and a nice job advising the Abbot of Crowland. He passed away peacefully in 1346 and is buried in Ashby Folville churchyard.

The final leg of this ride goes right on the road that comes out of Ashby Folville; then you continue straight ahead onto what is called locally the Gated Road. Head almost due east, then go left into Thorpe Satchville, and right on Bakers Lane.

You then go right on the first trail you see, cross Melton Lane, and head for the Iron Age fort at Burrough Hill Country Park. Archaeologists reckon that work to build the fort started around 3,000 years ago, but they have also found evidence of human habitation here going back at least 7,000 years. The area around the fort, including the car park that marks the start and finish of this ride, was the site of one of the UK's first towns, as people gathered around it to seek protection from the fort.

24 Hilly Lincs
Exploring the folds and furrows of the Lincolnshire Wolds

DIFFICULTY RATING **6/10** WILDNESS RATING **6/10**

If you think Lincolnshire is flat, come to the Wolds. They are the highest land in eastern England between Yorkshire and Kent, geologically an extension of the Yorkshire Wolds, which they most resemble in the north. This ride, though, is in the south Wolds, where their domed summits and deep folds contrast with the low fenland that surrounds them.

Horncastle bills itself as the 'Gateway to the Wolds', which is a fair description, since ecclesiastically Horncastle is part of the Fen and Hill Deanery. It's certainly the gateway to this ride. Start at the main A158/A153 crossroads near the centre of town and head south, going left after 3 kilometres. Head for Mareham-on-the-Hill, then Hameringham, where you turn left at the T-junction on the eastern edge of the village close to some trees.

The opening section is consistently uphill to a typical Wolds top, which are all up around the 120 to 140 metres mark. Turn right just past the radio mast for a short stretch east on the B1195, where when it's clear there's an incredible view south-east towards Boston and The Wash beyond.

Turn left onto a trail before reaching Winceby, and you continue climbing past the site of the English Civil War Battle of Winceby. According to legend Oliver Cromwell narrowly escaped death here when his horse was shot beneath him. However, Cromwell and the Parliamentarians still prevailed, and Royalist Lincolnshire fell to them by the end of this battle.

As you continue the trail deteriorates, and when I did this ride there was a gate to open and close just before the A158. After crossing the A158 the trail is a good solid farm track,

FACT FILE

Where Horncastle is 19 miles east of Lincoln using the A158

OS grid ref TF 2060 6955

Start/Finish Horncastle A158/A153 crossroads

Ride distance 22 kilometres (13.75 miles)

Highest point Fulletby (135 metres)

Approximate time 2–3 hours

with grass growing down the middle. The change is fortuitous, because this is the first consistent downhill section of the ride. It's steep in places, but flattens after 1.3 kilometres, just past a mound that looks man-made. You cross a tiny stream, then there's a short drag uphill to Ashby Puerorum. Its Latin suffix turns simple Ashby into Little Boy's Ashby, and was done by a 13th-century bishop, who used this parish's revenues to pay for the choir in Lincoln Cathedral.

Take the first left in Ashby, then keep left and continue to the T-junction with Tetford Road. Go left, then almost immediate right onto a

... continue climbing past the site of the English Civil War Battle of Winceby. According to legend Oliver Cromwell narrowly escaped death here when his horse was shot beneath him.

bridleway. It's a green and bumpy track at first, then improves for 20 metres in a grassy field, but be careful. Where the improved track swings right you must carry straight on, because the track has no right of way. Carry on across the field, go through a gap in the hedge and the bridleway improves, becoming more distinct.

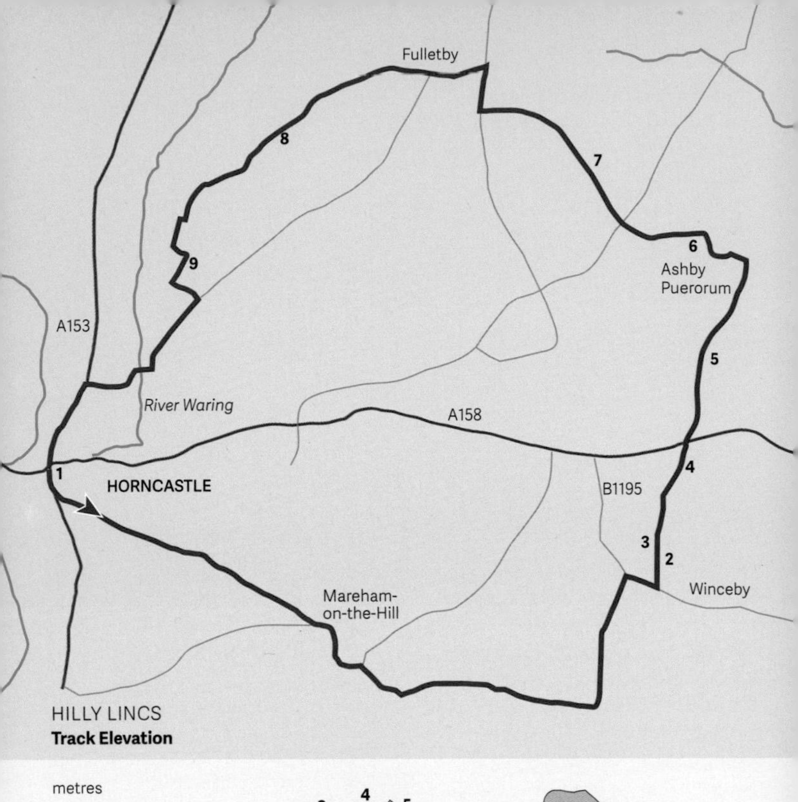

HILLY LINCS

Track Elevation

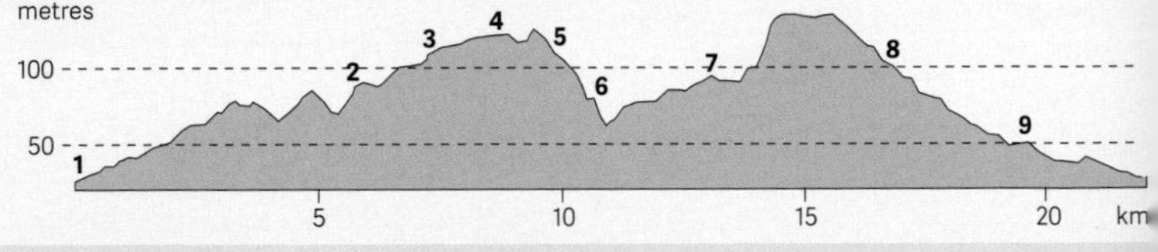

1 Start/Finish
2 First trail section
3 Battle of Winceby
4 Trail deteriorates
5 Long downhill
6 Left then almost immediately right
7 Trail indistinct in place
8 Downhill bumpy trail
9 Complicated navigation around field edges

Continue straight and you start to climb towards Hoe Hill, a Neolithic burial ground, where the track bends left, then goes right diagonally across a field, then sharp left to form a T-junction with a road. Go right on the road, then first left into Fulletby, the birthplace in 1816 of a country poet called Henry Winn.

Winn, who in a *Stamford Mercury* headline was once called 'The Grand Old Man of Lincolnshire', wrote about rural life in his native county, which was hard. His wife gave birth to 21 children during their marriage, but only four survived, a ratio at the top end of local experience but not unusual then. Winn managed to buck the survival odds of 19th-century rural England with his own life, and worked until his death in 1914, when he was 98.

Ride through Fulletby and go left onto a bridleway at a grass triangle where the road forks. Ride past Grange Farm. The surface is good at first, but turns green and bumpy. Take extra care, because this section is downhill almost all the way back to Horncastle. It requires good navigation, too.

The first place you could go wrong is where the farm track bends left. You must continue straight on the bumpy green section of the bridleway. Go between fields at first, one continuous one to the left and three different fields on your right. The trail then zig-zags in a series of right-angles around several more fields, before running parallel to, then going left to join, the Horncastle-to-Fulletby road.

Turn right onto the road, which is also part of the Viking Way, a long-distance footpath with plenty of cycling sections. It follows the path that Viking invaders took from the River Humber to the county of Rutland. Viking rule, called Danelaw, spread out from this path, and villages around it that end in 'by' are examples of Viking influence.

Turn left on the A153 and head south into Horncastle. Like all the rides in this book, this is just a sample of wild cycling in the Lincolnshire Wolds. There's a network of bridleways around Brinkhill, and another further north near Binbrook, while Lincolnshire also has some of the loveliest lanes in England.

25 Dales of Derbyshire

Exploring some well-known and less well-known valleys that make up the Derbyshire Dales

DIFFICULTY RATING **8/10** WILDNESS RATING **7/10**

This is quite a tough ride, but you experience what this very attractive part of the country has to explore. There are several places you could start the ride from, but I chose Monsal Head because it has a huge car park and has played a big part in local cycling history.

Monsal Head is the finish of a short but tough hill climb race that starts in the Wye Valley directly below it. The first Monsal Hill Climb was held in 1930, when C. Newell of the Sheffield Phoenix Cycling Club won in a time of 2 minutes 51 seconds for its 650 metres of 16% average gradient. The record fell every subsequent year until 'Lol' Dodds, also of the Sheffield Phoenix, broke the 90-second barrier with 1 minute 29.6 seconds in 1941. Dodds reduced that to 1 minute 24.3 in 1946, then Tom Simpson, the first non-Sheffield rider to hold the record, did 1 minute 23.4 seconds in 1957. That stood until Malcolm Elliott's stunning 1 minute 14.2 ride in 1981, and that was it. Elliott is from Sheffield, so civic pride was restored, and what is now the longest-standing British hill climb record was set.

Some sections of this ride are rough, so it's one for cyclo-cross, gravel or mountain bikes. Head down the hill and the road forks after 1.8 kilometres. You can go left, but going right takes you up a lovely little wooded valley. Climb to the hairpin, then descend, keep right and head for Litton. Go left in Litton, down Litton Dale, one of the shortest of the Derbyshire Dales, then turn left onto the B6049 to ride down the longer and lovely Tideswell Dale. Follow the B6049 until Miller's Dale Station, where you turn right to join the Monsal Trail.

This is a section of the former

FACT FILE

Where Monsal Head is in the Peak District, 18 kilometres west of Chesterfield and 2 kilometres north of Bakewell

OS grid ref SK 1848 7156

Start/Finish Monsal Head

Ride distance 32 kilometres (20 miles)

Highest point Hollow on the Moor (354 metres)

Approximate time 3–4 hours

Manchester-Buxton-Matlock railway that has been converted for use by cyclists and walkers. The Monsal Trail is ideal for exploring this part of Derbyshire without having to take on the hills. I have included a short section of it on this ride for three reasons. The first is to experience cycling through a long tunnel, which you do by following the trail west under Chee Tor to emerge in glorious Chee Dale, which is the second reason for using the Monsal Trail. Cross the Wye, then follow the trail a further kilometre to enjoy Chee Dale some more, then stop, turn around and ride back through the tunnel into Miller's Dale.

This is the third reason for this excursion. Miller's Dale is deep, heavily wooded and mysterious. Ride 2 kilometres east along the Monsal Trail until you are opposite Litton Mill. There's a little footbridge to it across the River Wye.

Litton Mill was an unprofitable 18th-century woollen mill that exploited child labour to keep costs down. The story of an orphan who worked here, Robert Blincoe, is thought to have been Charles Dickens' inspiration for *Oliver Twist*. Orphans suffered terrible conditions in mills like Litton, and legend goes that some other local mills are haunted by

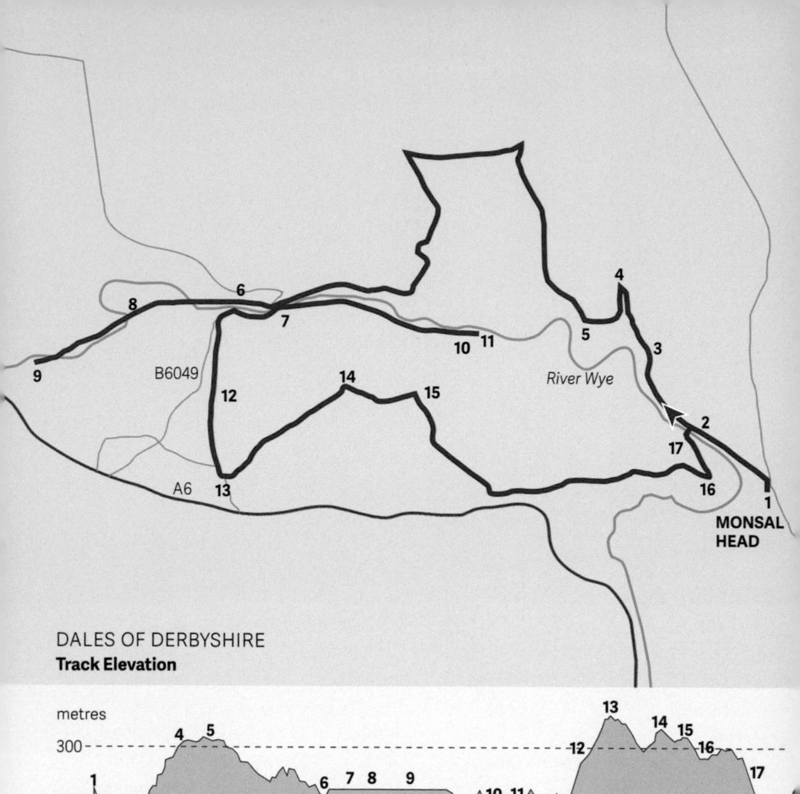

DALES OF DERBYSHIRE

Track Elevation

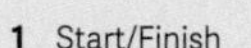

metres

300
200

5
10
15
20
25
km

1 2 3 4 5 6 7 8 9 10 11 12 13 14 15 16 17

1 Start/Finish
2 The Monsal hill climb
3 Right fork to climb up wooded valley
4 Hairpin bend
5 Keep right
6 Miller's Dale Station
7 Go west on Monsal Trail
8 Tunnel section
9 Chee Dale turnaround
10 Litton Mill
11 Miller's Dale turnaround
12 Long Lane
13 Hollow on the Moor
14 Sharp right
15 Sharp right
16 Trail becomes rough further down
17 Tricky descent

orphan ghosts. Miller's Dale is a lovely place today, but those children suffered appallingly and such things do leave their mark, if only on the mind.

Head back from Litton Mill to Miller's Dale Station, go left off the Trail onto the B6049, and after 500 metres look for Long Lane on your left. This is a long, straight and occasionally bumpy uphill trail to Hollow on the Moor, the highest point of this ride at 354 metres.

To continue the route you turn left at the top of the hill onto Priestcliffe Road, but if you crossed the busy A6 you'd be in Taddington, which at 1,100 feet above sea level is one of the highest villages in England. Quarries are the reason why this village grew up here. Some of them extract Ashford Marble, which is not a true marble but limestone with lots of muddy deposits and bitumen in it. It's very decorative when polished, and a favourite with sculptors.

Priestcliffe Road merges into an old road/trail called Broadway Lane, which leads to a disused mine. Follow Broadway Lane, but take the sharp right called Bulltor Lane before it gets to the mine. Ride over Bull Tor then down the edge of High Dale to Brushfield.

High Dale is a dry valley formed by meltwater after the Ice Age. The geology of this area is predominantly limestone, a porous rock, so where rivers flow in the deeper dales, like Miller's Dale, it's because erosion

Litton Mill was an unprofitable 18th-century woollen mill that exploited child labour to keep costs down. The story of an orphan who worked here, Robert Blincoe, is thought to have been Charles Dickens' inspiration for Oliver Twist.

---

has been sufficient to reveal older, impermeable rocks.

Go left at the farm buildings and continue straight where the road goes sharp right. That way you pick up a trail running along the edge of Monsal Dale, and it's quite spectacular. Enjoy the views early, though, because the trail gets very involving further down. You need your wits about you.

The trail weaves a bit as a warning, then there's a place where it divides. Veer left and follow this trail under the bridge that carries the Monsal Trail. Take great care on this downhill section: it's rough, and it might be better to walk the steepest bits if you aren't used to rough descents.

You eventually cross the River Wye, and come out on the road you used shortly after the start. You are at the foot of the Monsal Head hill climb, a bit ahead of the race start, but turn right and give it your best shot. The finish line is just in front of the café at the top, about halfway around the left-hand bend. Get your breath back and you can have a cuppa.

7

26 On My Doorstep

A spin around back lanes and bridleways I discovered as a kid, and still ride today

DIFFICULTY RATING **5/10** WILDNESS RATING **6/10**

I grew up in a coal-mining village in the north of England. Like most coal-mining villages it's surrounded by open countryside. Coal mining was rarely an urban industry: mines or collieries – pits, we called them – were sunk where the coal was, and where there was room to extract it. Communities were simply created to work there.

My village was Harworth; its colliery was sunk in 1913, and a village for miners called Bircotes was built next to it. Eventually the miners spread into both places, and Harworth and Bircotes became one, but the pit where my father and both grandfathers worked has gone. The spoil heaps have grass and trees growing on them now. One, which would smoulder and flare with patches of flame when it was windy, was moved to make way for a housing estate. The giant tower for the hauling gear was the last thing to go. It stood while the pit was demolished around it, but it succumbed to the dynamite men in 2016.

I know the countryside around Harworth like no other, because I cycled there as a kid. The pit tower, the spoil heaps: they were landmarks in a pre-GPS childhood. Harworth was where I built a sense of place, which all cyclists do if they stay anywhere for long. My bike meant freedom and exploration, and you never forget those early experiences.

That's why, after living in other parts of the UK for nearly 30 years, I now live close to the same network of back roads and trails I discovered as a kid. So this ride demonstrates what's on almost everybody's doorstep. It's not flashy or very adventurous; it's just a loop of bridleways and lanes you can find almost anywhere.

Start in Bawtry, so proud of its

FACT FILE

Where North Nottinghamshire, mostly south of the A631 Bawtry-to- Gainsborough road

OS grid ref SK 6509 9300

Start/Finish Bawtry

Ride distance 44 kilometres (27.5 miles)

Highest point Bridleway east of Hayton (58 metres)

Approximate time 3–4 hours

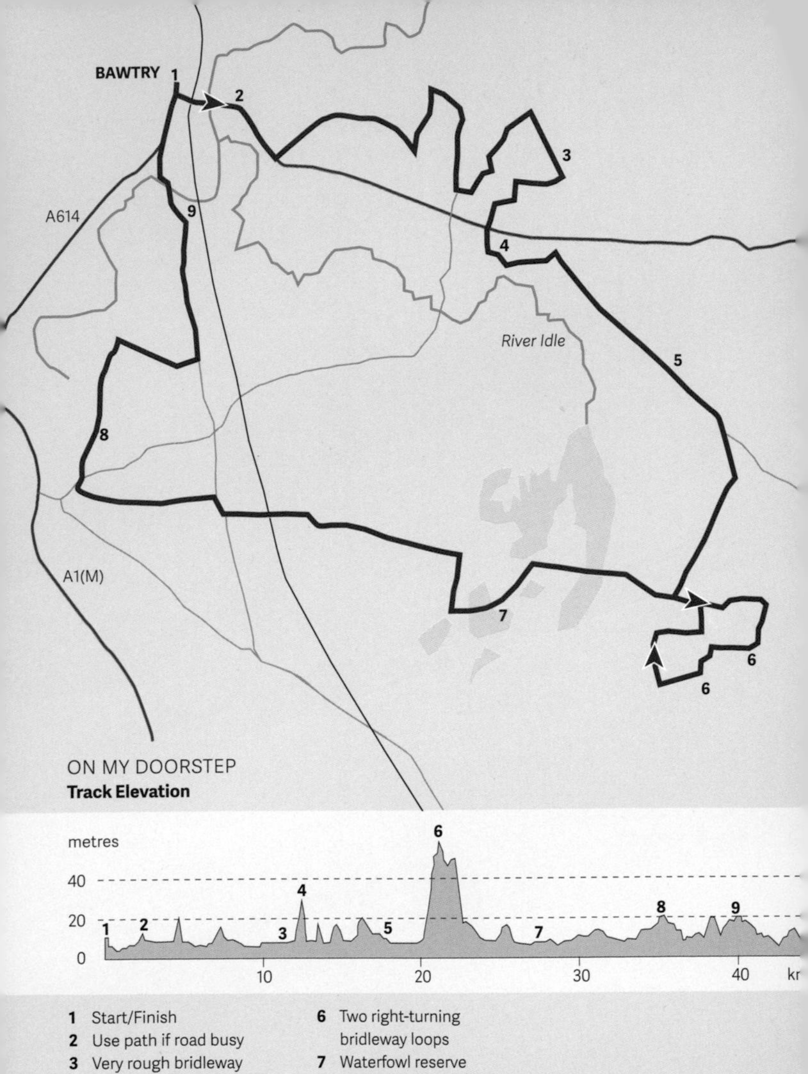

1 Start/Finish
2 Use path if road busy
3 Very rough bridleway
4 Shallow sandstone gorge
5 Long road section
6 Two right-turning bridleway loops
7 Waterfowl reserve
8 Roman bank
9 Site of Scrooby Manor

Yorkshireness that the address of the first house entering from the south is Number 1, Yorkshire. Bawtry is also a gateway to some rich farming country, a green and pleasant patchwork of fields and red-brick villages that glows with quiet country charm.

The first mile goes east along the busy A631. Harworth is 3 miles west of Bawtry, but the coal seam dips eastwards. For almost 100 years the coal face was pushed steadily along this road towards Gainsborough, but 1,000 metres below it. Use the path if you like for this bit; locals use it as an unofficial cycleway. Turn left onto a trail after the lay-by, and follow it around Harwell Wood to a road where you turn left.

The road quickly changes to trail; continue to the first right turn. Stop here, look back the way you came, and you'll see a low ridge that was once the edge of a glacial lake called Lake Humber. You would have been standing on the lake bed.

Take the right trail, go right again into Everton, then first left onto a trail that crosses Gringley Carr. A carr is a northern European ecosystem that is evolving from swamp to forest. Before the 1650s Gringley Carr and all the low flatland here was under water; then it was drained by the Dutch engineer Cornelius Vermuyden to create today's super-productive farmland. The whole area is criss-crossed by bridleways; some are the only way to lonely farms. A raised area of land, the Isle of Axholme, to the north-east, was an island before Vermuyden's work.

Still following trails, take the two right turns, the first section being quite heavy going, and head back towards Everton. Cross the A631 and follow the trail uphill, then go left at the top through a shallow sandstone gorge. This can get obstructed by fallen branches: take care when dismounting to step over them.

Join the road and go left to Drakeholes, where a tunnel takes the Chesterfield Canal through the ridge you just climbed over. There's a long stretch of flat road next through Clayworth to Hayton, where you go left after the hump-back bridge, then immediately right, to do a right-turning loop of bridleways east of the village. Turn left on reaching the road, and first right to another right-turning bridleway loop, this time west of Hayton.

Turn left on reaching the road again, and go back over the hump-back bridge, but continue straight where the road turns sharply right. This off-road section runs through the Idle Valley waterfowl reserve. The ponds are reclaimed gravel pits.

Take the first right after the trail becomes road. Turn left towards Torworth, then right at the T-junction, and almost immediately left in the village. Then go right where this road forks. Turn right on the B6045 towards Ranskill, but after 100 metres turn left

... Scrooby Manor was home to William Brewster, one of the Pilgrim Fathers who in 1620 sailed to America on the Mayflower.

onto a bridleway that follows an old Roman bank. Turn right at the second road, the one coming out of Serlby Park. This was the Duke of Galway's gaff, the most northerly of the homes that make up the Dukeries. It's in private hands today.

After a mile you get to a main road, the old A1, or Great North Road as it was known before roads had numbers. It's wide and fairly traffic-free now: the A1(M) a few miles west has seen to that. Turn left onto the Great North Road and head back to Bawtry, diverting right through Scrooby.

This was an important place on the Great North Road, and Scrooby Manor was home to William Brewster, one of the Pilgrim Fathers who in 1620 sailed to America on the *Mayflower*. Continue north on the little lane through Scrooby, crossing the River Ryton, and turn right on the North Road for the last mile back to Bawtry.

I hope you enjoy this ride. Most of us don't live among jaw-dropping splendour. We live where we live, and we mostly ride in what's outside our front door. This is what's outside mine: what's outside yours?

27 Abandoned Road

Wrecked by landslides, the old Mam Tor road makes an excellent springboard for a Peak District adventure

DIFFICULTY RATING **7/10** WILDNESS RATING **8/10**

Mam Tor is one of the great landmarks of the Peak District. Part of a ridge of hills rising near Chapel-en-le-Frith that runs east to the River Derwent at Bamford, it is the stand-out feature in the Hope Valley, where Mam Tor shows its scarred but very beautiful face.

The scar gives Mam Tor its other two names. The Shivering Mountain is one, because around 4,000 years ago the whole south-eastern side of Mam Tor slid into the Hope Valley, leaving an unstable cliff that has been crumbling ever since. Some of the larger fallen sections formed baby hills beneath the cliff, hence Mam Tor's third name, the Mother Hill.

A main road connecting the Hope Valley with Chapel-en-le-Frith once clambered over the shoulder of Mam Tor, doing a big switchback across its south-eastern flank. The switchback lessened the gradient, providing a way for heavy vehicles. Go a kilometre further south, and Winnats Pass shows how steep the gradient would have been. But the main road was continuously damaged by landslips, and it was abandoned in 1979.

Or at least, it was abandoned by motor vehicles. Mam Tor's shattered old road now provides cyclists with an excellent springboard for adventure, which this ride uses to explore both faces of the Peak District, the Dark and the White Peaks.

Start in Castleton, and head west towards Winnats Pass. After 500 metres you fork right to start climbing up the abandoned road. In fine weather there'll be daredevil paragliders flinging themselves from the top of Mam Tor, swooping down into the void to gain speed, then soaring up into the thermals above

FACT FILE

Where Almost mid-way between Manchester and Sheffield

OS grid ref SK 1517 8293

Start/Finish Castleton

Ride distance 32 kilometres (20 miles)

Highest points Lord's Seat (550 metres), Limestone Way above Oxlow Rake (450 metres)

Approximate time 2–3 hours

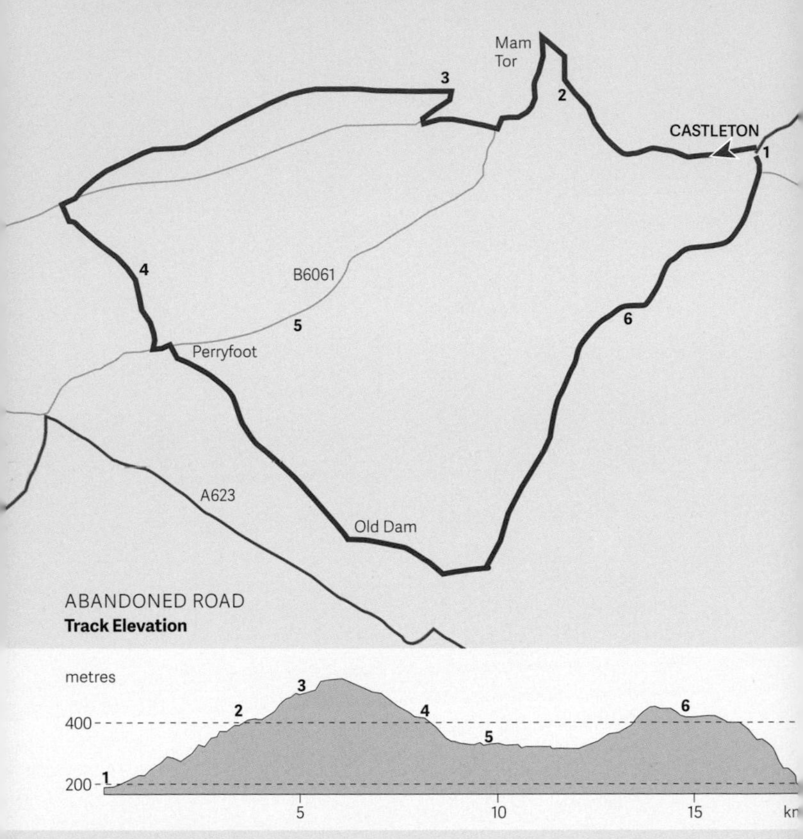

1 Start/Finish. Lots of car parks in Castleton
2 Start of shattered section of abandoned road
3 Start of Rushup bridleway on left before top of Mam Nick Pass
4 No Car Café
5 Short cut if required
6 Trail fork, go right

you. It looks fantastic, and terrifying.

Staying on the bike all the way to the top is a challenge, but doing so is mountain-bike territory really. The road is so shattered in places it looks like an earthquake hit it. Best to dismount and walk around the worst bits. You have plenty of time. Wild cycling is about freedom, the feel of riding where others don't go, but above all it's about the landscape. The view from the top of the abandoned road is breathtaking. The whole sway of the Hope Valley spreads out before you, all the way to the gritstone edges in the east.

Resume riding and continue west along the road, signposted Chapel-en-le-Frith, and you pass a feature on your left called Windy Knoll. It was once part of a coral reef in an ancient sea, and underneath it there's a cave where Victorian archaeologists unearthed the bones of reindeer, bison and wolves.

Ride a further 500 metres along the road then take the right turn, almost back on yourself, signposted Edale, and climb towards the pass between Mam Tor and Rushup Edge. You turn left near the top of the pass onto a bridleway that climbs up onto Rushup Edge. The pass itself is the finish line of the Mam Nick hill climb out of Edale, a classic that was recently revived by Sheffield's Rutland Cycling Club.

Surrounded by big cities, the Peak District is a magnet for cyclists, and always has been. As soon as cycling became more accessible during the first part of the 20th century, clubs full of miners, steelworkers and other heavy industries came here to explore and revel in the natural beauty, relax and enjoy the fresh air. The pull was even stronger for competitive individuals, and racing cyclists still train here in their thousands.

Shortly after I did this ride the next section was closed for repair, but the Peak District National Park Authority says it should be open by the time this book is published. If it's not, you can divert around this bit by going straight on after Windy Knoll, and pick up this ride again by turning left on the first road you get to.

The bridleway from the Mam Nick Pass to the top of Rushup Edge is quite steep at first and the surface loose in places, so take care. It might be best to dismount and push your bike up the steepest bits. It's about 1.5 kilometres in all to the summit at Lord's Seat, but riding along the elongated top and down to the next road section is a pure joy. Take care, though: the view is spectacular but the trail still demands attention.

Turn right where the bridleway meets the road, then take the next left, Rushup Lane. You go steeply downhill. Look out for the No Car Café, a specialist walkers' and cyclists' café on your left. It's worth visiting just to support their noble 'no car' business, but it's ideally placed on this

ride for a quick break and some extra sustenance.

The descent leads to Perryfoot, where you go left, then first right, onto a delightful little lane that runs through Perry Dale. Switching from abandoned roads to bridleway to tiny lanes is the essence of wild cycling, and this ride has them all. You reach the next bridleway by continuing straight through Old Dam, and it's one of the finest trails in the country. It's called the Limestone Way, an 80-kilometre high-level route through the White Peak. Riding its bridleway sections is a joy that this ride provides a small taste of.

Turn left onto the Limestone Way, and there's a steep climb with terrific views all the way up. The valley on your left is Oxlow Rake, while on your right is a wide expanse of upland limestone. It's all green airy spaces up here, with rocky outcrops and occasional clay ponds for livestock to drink from.

Take the right fork where the trail splits, because the other fork is a footpath. The bridleway follows a distinct dry valley called Secret Valley into Cave Dale. It's quite easy to pick out, and in no time you'll emerge at Bargate in Castleton, almost under the walls of the ancient but striking Peveril Castle. Be careful on the last 2.5 kilometres of downhill: it's very steep, and the surface is loose in three distinct places. Walking the steeper sections is the better part of valour.

28 Back o't' Moss

Holme Moss by the back way, then a mostly trail ride around the landscape of the West Yorkshire Pennines

DIFFICULTY RATING **8/10** WILDNESS RATING **8/10**

Cycling is full of iconic places made so by the races on them, and no race creates more icons than the Tour de France. Holme Moss was already famous in British cycling before the Tour climbed it in 2014; now it's famous the world over.

Holme Moss dominates this ride. It glowers over Ramsden Reservoir car park, one of many car parks you could start this ride from. It's a small one, though, so if it's full, drop down through Holmbridge into Holmfirth and park there – just return to the start by riding back up to Ramsden Reservoir.

If the reservoir and surrounding hills and woods seem familiar, they should be. This is where a succession of old men, starting with Compo, Clegg and Blamire back in 1973, got up to all kinds of tricks in the *Last of the Summer Wine* TV series. It was written by a former Doncaster policeman, Roy Clarke, and it ran and ran, and ran some more, until it became the longest-running TV sitcom ever. This area is now known as Summer Wine Country.

Turn left at the car park exit and follow the track between Ramsden and Riding Wood Reservoir, then climb through Holme Woods. Continue to a trail fork. Choose either branch, but the left one is very steep. Both join the road going over Holme Moss about halfway up. Turn left and pedal over Holme Moss. The radio transmitter at the summit is the highest in England. Take care: it can be windy up there.

The descent is long and flowing – great if you are comfortable with speed, although there are some dips in the road that can catch out the reckless. Road descents like this are thrilling, but keep speed within your comfort zone by prudent braking. The final dip has a right-hand bend and a steep climb coming out of it.

FACT FILE

Where The northern edge of the Dark Peak, halfway between Greater Manchester and Barnsley, and just south of Holmfirth

OS grid ref SE 1152 0565

Start/Finish Ramsden Reservoir car park

Ride distance 37.5 kilometres (23.5 miles)

Highest point Holme Moss (524 metres)

Approximate time 4–5 hours

You end up in Longdendale, at the foot of one of the oldest ways across the Pennines, the Woodhead Pass. It can look dark and forbidding, especially in winter when the valley's crags seem to wrinkle like a frown. They look especially severe with a dusting of snow.

Go left, then leave the busy A628 after 200 metres on a trail that goes up the side of Pikenaze Moor. You have to cross the A628 twice while following this off-road track. After the second crossing head north-east on a metalled lane, looking for a large round structure on your left. It's an air shaft that helped ventilate the Woodhead Tunnel. It's closed now, but used to take the main line between Sheffield and Manchester.

Turn right when you spot the air shaft, and follow a bridleway that is part of the Barnsley Boundary Walk. The South Yorkshire town isn't immediately associated with wild moorland like this, but it stands right on the edge of the Pennines. The coal seam that Barnsley is better known for starts in these hills. A couple of miles further east you will see black scars of the first mines poking like grazes through the landscape's thin skin.

The Boundary Walk crosses the A628 once more. Follow the main trail past Langsett Reservoir to a car park

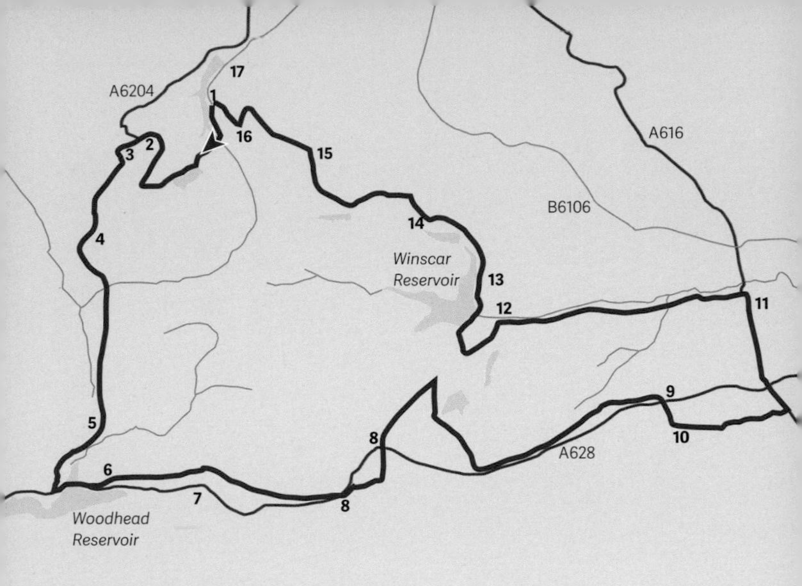

BACK O'T' MOSS

Track Elevation

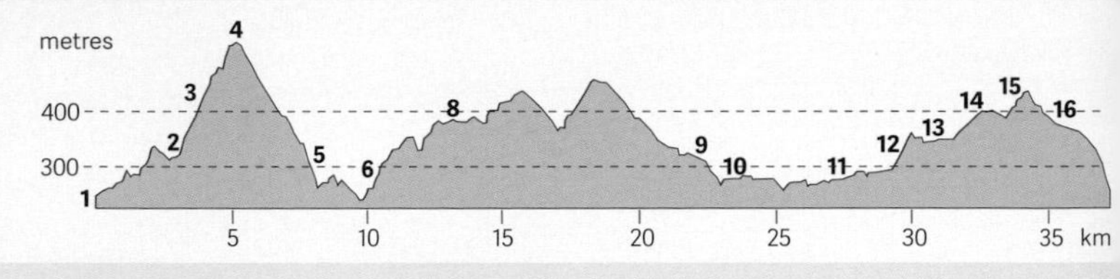

1 Start/Finish

2 Trail fork

3 Climb of Holme Moss

4 Car park, highest point of ride

5 Sudden dips in the descent, take care

6 Very steep uphill

7 Woodhead Pass

8 Two busy road crossings, take care

9 Road crossing

10 Straight past Langsett Reservoir

11 Follow Trans-Pennine Trail west

12 Woodhead Tunnel

13 Car park

14 Harden Clough

15 Trail intersects road

16 Zig-zag descent

17 Follow this road north-east for Holmfirth

where you go left on the A616, then straight on at the roundabout. Now look for signs for the Trans-Pennine Cycle Route on your left. It's a fantastic route that starts in Hornsea on the east coast, and crosses the country to Southport on the west. It offers a variety of wild and urban back-road cycling along the way.

The section of the trail you use goes west to the mouth of Woodhead Tunnel. There's a lot of history here: 250 steam trains a day used to pass through this tunnel. It must have been a sensory overload of hissing steam, thick smoke and coal sparks as trains puffed and panted on the long pull from Sheffield to the tunnel. And it must have looked even more spectacular when they exploded out of the tunnel mouth at speed the other way.

It's a lonely, eerie place now, with very little sun, and the memory of all those who died digging the tunnel adds to the shiver. There are three tunnels, each 3 miles long; 26 people were lost in completing tunnel one. Many more died constructing tunnel two, including 28 in an outbreak of cholera. It's a shame that, after all that human cost, the tunnels today are merely conduits for electricity cables, when reopening them for rail could help transport infrastructure here a lot.

Turn left onto the road and climb a steep hill, then go right to cross Winscar Reservoir dam and climb up to the road, where you go left. There's

an off-road alternative to be had on the uphill by following a trail on the left through the quarries of Harden Clough.

The stream flowing into the thinnest end of Winscar Reservoir is the infant Don, a river that christened an industry. From here the Don heads through Penistone, then Deepcar, where the steelworks start, then into Sheffield. The Don Valley is slowly being redeveloped today as a place for retail and leisure, but although some steel is still produced here, molten metal was once the red-hot blood that gave Sheffield life, making the city famous throughout the world.

Once on the road beyond Winscar/ Harden Clough, look for a trail that intersects it and take the left branch. This goes straight and level at first, but quickly becomes a brilliant little zig-zag off-road descent back to the start. It's lots of fun, especially in the last wooded bit at the bottom, but treat slippery tree roots with respect. If you are hungry there are loads of cafés in nearby Holmfirth.

29 Happy Valley to Brontëland

Two contrasting faces of Yorkshire's Calder Valley

DIFFICULTY RATING **8/10** WILDNESS RATING **8/10**

Hebden Bridge has seen massive change. It grew through the wool trade, but then many people moved away when the woollen mills closed through the 1970s. And when they did, property in Hebden became laughably cheap. So cheap that a wave of hippies, artists, musicians and new-agers moved in. Hebden became exotic, then trendy, and now it's chic. Property prices have rocketed, and although Hebden Bridge is still a very vital place, it is becoming increasingly dormitory. However, it's still very handsome, and very interesting.

It's certainly one of the jollier places in Calderdale, whose grittier side is portrayed in Sally Wainwright's TV series *Happy Valley*. But even through that riveting and sometimes shocking fiction Calderdale's stark beauty shines through. This ride takes in a lot of that beauty, as well as meeting, at a distance, one of this area's other great literary connections, the Brontë sisters.

Start at the Hebden Picture House, a well-known local landmark on the main A646 running through the Calder Valley. Head east on the main road for 500 metres, then turn left on the A6033, which is signposted Haworth. Head up this road for one kilometre then go left on Midgehole Road, following signs to Hardcastle Crags.

Turn right into Hardcastle Crags car park, continue north through the car park and follow a bridleway that climbs steeply up the bottom end of Crimsworth Dean. Unfortunately, the bridleway doesn't go all the way up this valley, because after 500 metres the right of way changes to footpath. However, where it changes another bridleway joins from your left. Go left on that bridleway, which

FACT FILE

Where Hebden Bridge is in West Yorkshire, 10 kilometres west of Halifax and 16 kilometres south-east of Burnley

OS grid ref SD 9891 2719

Start/Finish Hebden Picture House

Ride distance 21 kilometres (13.1 miles)

Highest point Heptonstall Moor (397 metres)

Approximate time 2–3 hours

These dark waters sit between Black Moor and Heptonstall Moor, creating an eerie location that attracted an occult group from Bradford called the Temple of Horrors.

eventually becomes Cow Hey Lane.

This is the start of a really enjoyable off-road stretch that goes up the valley of Hebden Water, but above it and following its contours. There aren't many changes of gradient for almost 4 kilometres, plenty of time to observe Calderdale's gaunt beauty. There are changes of trail surface, though. There's a long rough section after a kilometre, then a very rutted one at 3 kilometres, where Cow Hey becomes Kiln Lane.

Thankfully, that doesn't last long. You pass a splendid modern house, then descend to cross Alcomden Water, one of two tributary streams that join to form Hebden Water. There are two bridges across the stream: use the left one, because the right bridge has a gate after it.

The trail then climbs away from Alcomden Water, and you reach a triangle of trails. Turn left, but before you do, stop and look up the Alcomden Valley. The highest hill you see at the

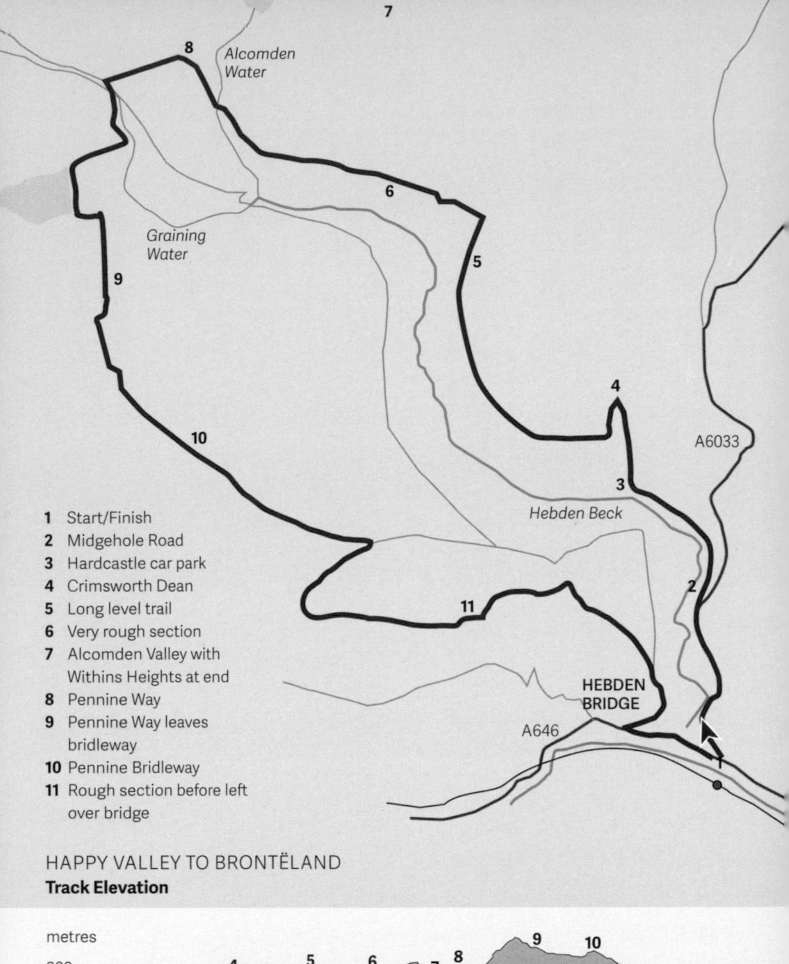

HAPPY VALLEY TO BRONTËLAND

Track Elevation

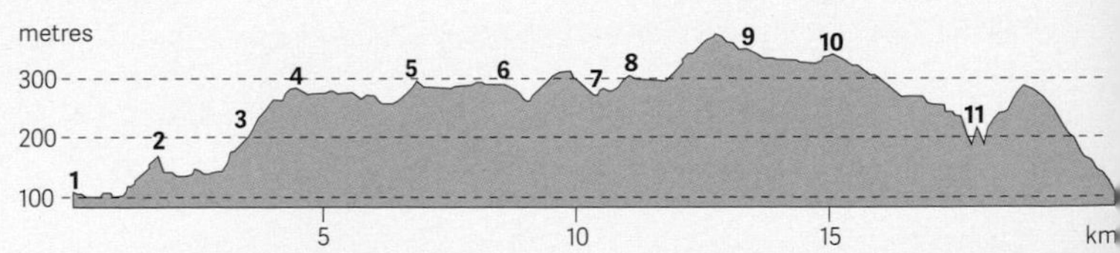

far end of the valley is called Withens Heights. On the other side of that there's an abandoned farmhouse called Top Withens. Both the hill and house are thought to have inspired the title of Emily Brontë's novel *Wuthering Heights*.

Turn left again and you are on the Pennine Way, where the Pennine Bridleway shares the footpath. Turn left onto a narrow road, then go almost immediately right over the bridge that crosses Hebden Water's other tributary, Graining Water.

Follow the trail south over the dam wall, across the lower of the two Gorple Reservoirs. These dark waters sit between Black Moor and Heptonstall Moor, creating an eerie location that attracted an occult group from Bradford called the Temple of Horrors. The group was full of professional people, including architects who were involved in the reservoirs' construction. It's not certain, but a good guess, that they carved the likeness of an Egyptian God on a big boulder beside a footpath here. It's one of many 'archaic heads' carved around the Calder Valley.

Turn left immediately after the dam, then first right to ride directly up the side of the valley. Continue south through the gate where the Pennine Way footpath goes off left. You carry on south following the Pennine Bridleway, then south-east where it becomes Edge Lane.

The Pennine Bridleway extends

from Derbyshire to Cumbria for 330 kilometres (205 miles), including two loops. One is the Settle Loop in the Yorkshire Dales, the other is here in the Calder Valley, the Mary Towneley Loop. It's 76 kilometres (47 miles), and should be on every wild-cycling bucket list. As should the Pennine Bridleway itself.

The Pennine Bridleway continues down to Hebden Bridge, and that makes a nice short cut for this ride, but to complete it you go right in Colden on Smithy Lane. Descend to Jack's Bridge. Go left immediately after the bridge onto Hudson Mill Road, and continue down a bumpy bridleway to Heptonstall, where the poet Sylvia Plath is buried in St Thomas's graveyard.

For the final section, turn left over the bridge onto Lumb Lane where the trail begins to swing right. Lumb Lane becomes Green Lane; turn right at the T-junction onto Town Gate and descend to Hebden Bridge, where you go left on the A646 to finish.

30 Escape the Conurbation

A short ride with a very steep climb that has a bit of almost everything

DIFFICULTY RATING **8/10** WILDNESS RATING **5/10**

The conurbation in question is the Leeds-to-Keighley built-up strip along the Aire Valley, and this ride proves that wild-cycling opportunities exist in unexpected places if you look for them. Part of the ride follows a canal towpath, part of it crosses parkland and open-country areas where there are rights of way. You often find parkland in urban areas, but one thing probably restricted to the north is the long cobbled-road section on this ride. Cobbled roads are a boon to wild cycling because motorists avoid them, and they have a special place in the sport of cycling, but more of that later.

I was shown this ride by a cyclo-cross racer who grew up in the area, using bits of it to hone his skills and fitness. His name is Chris Young: he was a national champion and a Three Peaks cyclo-cross winner, and they don't come wilder than that.

The ride uses trails with some loose surfaces and roads, and includes flat bits, climbs and descents. You can do it on almost any bike, so long as it has good thick tyres.

It starts on the Leeds–Liverpool canal towpath in Bingley at the Three-Rise Locks, close to Damart Mill. You gain access to the locks from Hillside Road in Bingley. Cross the canal just above the top lock and head north on the towpath. This section is part of the Aire Valley Towpath, a great place for family rides –www.airevalleytowpath.org. The towpath can also be used to access more adventurous rides in the Yorkshire Dales.

After 400 metres you reach Bingley Five-Rise Locks, the steepest rise on the British canal network. The locks lift barges up 18.03 metres in 98 metres of canal, a gradient of 20%. Because they are so complicated, a full-time lock keeper has to take boats through. The Five-Rise was completed

FACT FILE

Where Bingley is 8 kilometres north-west of Bradford city centre

OS grid ref SE 1036 3952

Start/Finish Bingley Three-Rise Locks

Ride distance 13.2 kilometres (8.25 miles)

Highest point Start of Alter Lane (272 metres)

Approximate time 1–2 hours

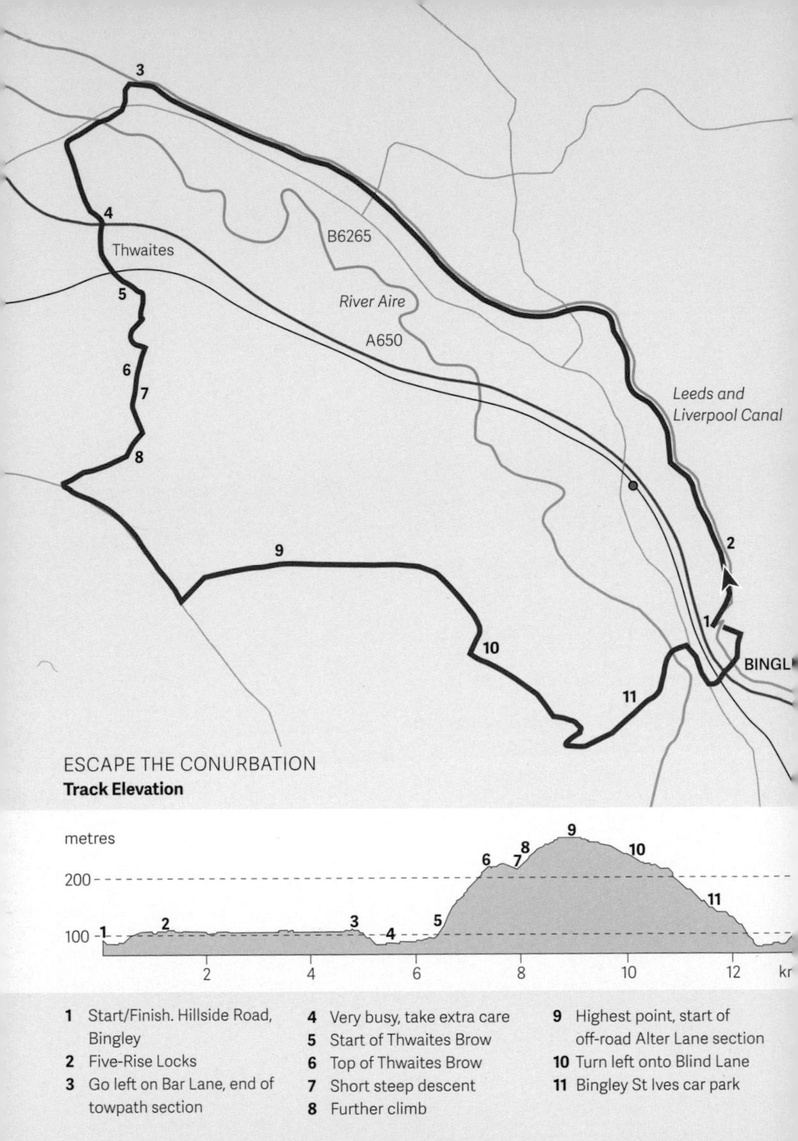

3
4
Thwaites
5
6
7
8
9
10
11
B6265
River Aire
A650
Leeds and
Liverpool Canal
2
1
BINGL
ESCAPE THE CONURBATION
Track Elevation
metres
200
100
2
4
6
8
10
12
km
1 Start/Finish. Hillside Road, Bingley
2 Five-Rise Locks
3 Go left on Bar Lane, end of towpath section
4 Very busy, take extra care
5 Start of Thwaites Brow
6 Top of Thwaites Brow
7 Short steep descent
8 Further climb
9 Highest point, start of off-road Alter Lane section
10 Turn left onto Blind Lane
11 Bingley St Ives car park

in 1774, and is a terrific feat of canal engineering.

Continue along the towpath for another 4.5 kilometres, until it crosses Bar Lane in Riddlesden. Turn left onto Bar Lane, then go right on the busy B6265, and after 400 metres turn left onto Airworth Road. Follow this south to cross the big A650 roundabout, taking the third exit, Wenning Street, with great care. This the busiest part of this ride, but including it is essential, otherwise it would just be a ride up and down a canal towpath.

Go straight across the junction with Valley Road and Dalton Lane, over Thwaites Bridge, then turn left onto Thwaites Brow Road. Strap yourself in: the next bit is 'character-building', which is what people say when they mean horrible.

Actually, I don't mean horrible: if you are a real cyclist you'll be thrilled by the climb of Thwaites Brow. It is 1,000 metres long, and averages 12.6% gradient, but the first part is more like 25%, and its surface is cobblestones: wicked, laughing, slippery cobblestones. But cobblestones have a special place in cyclists' hearts.

Cobbled roads are the big feature of races called the northern Classics, in particular Paris-Roubaix and the Tour of Flanders. Even more applicable to Thwaites Brow, cobbled climbs are the big feature of the Tour of Flanders, but even in that race there is nothing as fearsome as Thwaites Brow.

... the next bit is 'character-building', which is what people say when they mean horrible.

Think about that when you get to the summit; it will make you proud.

The classic advice for climbing cobbled roads is to sit in the saddle as much as possible, so your weight over the rear wheel improves its traction. Shift to your lowest gear at the bottom of Thwaites Brow, and stay in it until the gradient relents. You might still have to get out of the saddle to muster enough power down on the steepest section. Just don't move your body too far forward when you do.

There's a short, steep descent after the official top of Thwaites Brow, but the road quickly goes up again for another kilometre, during which you turn left. Go left again at the top of the hill and onto the next trail section, which is called Alter Lane. It runs along the edge of a golf course, and a network of trails goes off it. Take the first one right just before a local landmark called Druid's Alter.

Follow this trail around a 90-degree right bend and, soon after the trail straightens, go left onto a tree-lined trail called Blind Lane. Still descending, this becomes a road at Bingley St Ives car park and leads to the B6429. Turn left, and descend to cross the River Aire. Go right onto the B6265, then first left into Bingley, and back to the start.

31 Wonderful Wolds

An exploration of the shapely valleys and wide-open tops of the Yorkshire Wolds

DIFFICULTY RATING **7/10** WILDNESS RATING **7/10**

The Yorkshire Wolds is a bright and breezy region with a very distinctive landscape. It's a chalk upland that forms an arc from the River Humber just west of Hull to Bridlington on the Yorkshire coast. Wolds valleys are deep, dry and short: you come across them suddenly as green slashes in an undulating plateau. The arable fields are on top of the Wolds, with livestock grazing in the valleys. It's an upside-down way of farming that makes these hills look like a patchwork quilt that's been carelessly tossed aside.

There are rides using old ways across the tops and through valleys all over the Yorkshire Wolds, and because chalk is porous the Wolds are well drained, so the bridleways and green lanes are more often dry than muddy. However, when chalky soils get wet they get really gloopy.

Start from Huggate, go south on the main street, then turn right. Turn right again as you leave the village. After 1,600 metres there is a green bridleway on your left. It's a bit bumpy in places and leads to a small lane, and the first Wolds valley on this ride. Turn right and ride down the valley.

In just over 2 kilometres there's a bridleway on your right that climbs up another valley: follow it north. It's a green lane at first and a bit bumpy, but when you reach a conifer plantation the trail is more like a fire road.

The trail section lasts 3 kilometres, and is uphill most of the way. Turn left when you reach a road at the top of the valley, then left on the next road, which crosses the top of High Callis Wold. This is a good section to look around and get the feel of what the Wold tops look like.

Seven hundred metres after two masts at the top of the Wold, turn left

FACT FILE

Where This part of the Yorkshire Wolds is 25 kilometres east of York

OS grid ref SE 8817 5506

Start/Finish Huggate.

Ride distance 21.5 kilometres (13.4 miles)

Highest point High Callis Wold (233 metres)

Approximate time 2–3 hours

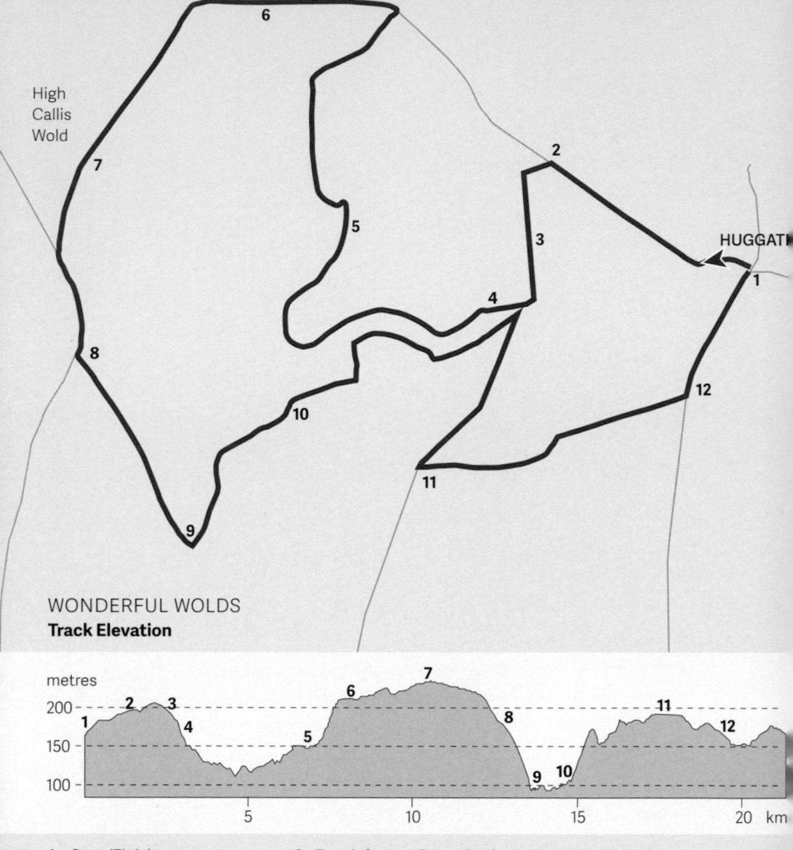

1 Start/Finish
2 Left onto bridleway
3 Bumpy bridleway
4 Steep downhill road section in first valley
5 Long uphill trail, very steep in places
6 Long road section
7 Highest point of ride
8 Turn left onto Green Bank
9 Turn left on road up valley
10 Turn right, very steep off-road uphill
11 Turn left for last off-road section
12 Turn left onto road to Huggate

The arable fields are on top of the Wolds, with livestock grazing in the valleys. It's an upside-down way of farming that makes these hills look like a patchwork quilt that's been carelessly tossed aside.

onto Green Bank, a bridleway that follows the course of a Roman road. This section goes steeply downhill, and ends at the road going up the first valley you entered. Turn left, then after 1,200 metres go right onto a bridleway. This is very steep as it goes up the side of a valley, but the gradient quickly relents as you ride around the edge of a small copse. The trail is green and bumpy and vague at first, but becomes flatter and more distinct later. Turn right on the road at the end of it, then after 1,300 metres go left into the last bridleway section. This is hard-packed earth at first but greener later, and it links the tops of two valleys. Turn left on the road at the end and ride back to Huggate.

There: that's a sample of the Yorkshire Wolds, a bright landscape bathed in a special light that has inspired the artist David Hockney and the writer Winifred Holtby, among many others.

32 The John Rawnsley

A ride in the Yorkshire Dales dedicated to the creator of a famous British bike race

DIFFICULTY RATING **7/10** WILDNESS RATING **8/10**

The Three Peaks Cyclo-Cross is the hardest cyclo-cross race in the world. The Three Peaks in question are Ingleborough, Whernside and Pen-y-ghent, a classic walkers' route since 1887. The muscular symmetry of combining them in one route captured the imaginations of many, but none more so than a former Bradford accountant called John Rawnsley.

He organised and won the first Three Peaks Cyclo-Cross, and until recently held its participation record at 45 times. He also ran the Three Peaks fell race 30 times, and by now must have completed the route getting on for 200 times, walking, running or riding. He's a supreme endurance athlete who has accomplished many other challenges, but the Three Peaks is his fascination.

The route was already well known to runners through the Three Peaks fell race when, in September 1959, a Skipton schoolboy, Kevin Watson, cycled it. Rawnsley read about his feat in the local paper, and it inspired him, so with a few Bradford cycling mates he decided to try it in 1960.

The group – Harry Bond, Geoff Whittam, Ron Bows, Pete O'Neil and Rawnsley – started in Ribblehead and climbed Whernside first, then Ingleborough then Pen-y-ghent. Intermediate times, punctures and falls, all are recorded in Rawnsley's meticulous diaries, as was their final time: 4 hours 31 minutes and 31 seconds for the full off-road 40 kilometres of the walkers' route. Then they got competitive.

'We did it again in May 1961,' Rawnsley remembers, 'and lowered the time to 3 hours 54 minutes, and we organised the first Three Peaks race on 1 October 1961. There were 35 starters, including a world championship cyclo-cross rider, Bill Radford from the Midlands. We went the same

FACT FILE

Where Central Yorkshire Dales

OS grid ref SD 9262 7818

Start/Finish Hubberholme

Ride distance 37 kilometres (23 miles)

Highest points Birkwith Moor (394 metres), Kidhow (517 metres)

Approximate time 3–4 hours

THE JOHN RAWNSLEY
Track Elevation

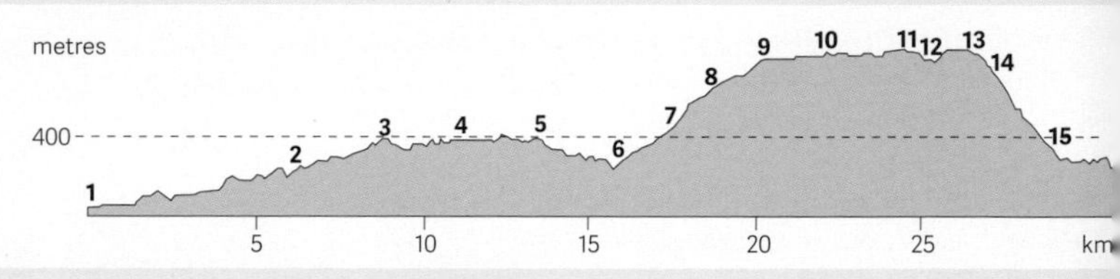

1 Start/Finish
2 Continue straight at this junction
3 Rough surfaced road
4 Road becomes trail
5 Start of short footpath section
6 End of footpath, start of rideable trail
7 Ling Gill
8 Cam End
9 Surface change to farm road
10 Kidhow
11 Long flat section
12 Turn right
13 Fleet Moss bog
14 Begin Fleet Moss descent
15 Very steep section

way as the fell race, Pen-y-ghent, then Whernside, then Ingleborough, starting and finishing in Horton-in-Ribblesdale. I won from Harry Bond.'

The Three Peaks Cyclo-Cross is massive now, and many hopefuls are disappointed each year because places are limited to those who can prove their ability to cope with it. It's the ultimate challenge for wild cycling as a sport, which is what it can be if you like the raw exhilaration of a race.

Rawnsley continued challenging for victory throughout the 1960s, and was always up front in his age group in later years. He doesn't take part now because of health issues, and he stopped organising the race in 2012 after 50 years.

In 2011 Rawnsley showed me this wild ride, which he used when he was training to race in the Three Peaks. It's not on the race route: the course for that, now much longer because of changes, only opens once a year for the race. It's mostly on private land and trails where wheeled vehicles aren't allowed. This ride is not nearly as hard as the Three Peaks, which has some extreme climbing and descents, but it provides a taste, and is worth doing on its own merits, because the Yorkshire Dales are a wonderful place.

You could start from a number of places. Beckermonds makes the ride a continuous loop, and there are car parks on or near the ride you could use. But I wanted to start at Hubberholme when I did this ride, which means an out-and-back ride along Langstrothdale to and from Beckermonds. I did it because I wanted to visit the grave of Yorkshire writer and playwright J. B. Priestley in Hubberholme churchyard.

Priestley was influential as well as a great writer. His Second World War radio broadcasts attracted 12 million listeners; only Winston Churchill got more. And Priestley's 1934 travelogue, *English Journey*, inspired George Orwell's *The Road to Wigan Pier*. They were catalysts for bringing social reform for a poorly treated working class.

Hubberholme is east of Beckermonds, so head west: there's only one road along Langstrothdale and it is rather lovely. Go straight through tiny Beckermonds, which is at the confluence of Oughtershaw Beck and Greenfield Beck, so it's where the River Wharfe starts. However, Wharfedale begins only after the river bends sharp right after Hubberholme.

Follow Greenfield Beck, still heading west, on a rough road that becomes an un-surfaced trail where woodland on either side closes to meet it. You can follow this trail to Horton-in-Ribblesdale, which opens up other wild-cycling possibilities. The Yorkshire Dales is a great place for wild cycling, and has a tradition of it. Yorkshire cycling clubs and individuals have always explored the extensive network of bridleways and

fi'zi:k

green roads up here by bike.

For this ride, though, you must look for a footpath on your right a kilometre after breaking out of the woodland. The footpath section is less than 800 metres long; it connects with Cam Fell High Road, and you should walk the short footpath section. Anyway, it's a nice opportunity to absorb the scenery.

Turn right when you meet Cam Fell High Road, which is a rough trail at this point, and follow it towards Cam End. Look west on this section and you can see Whernside and the Ribblehead Viaduct. After 2 kilometres you cross the top of Ling Gill, described by Alfred Wainwright as one of Yorkshire's finest limestone gorges, by an old packhorse bridge. The gorge is thought to be a collapsed cavern formed by Cam Beck. Its steep sides mean sheep can't graze them, so the gorge is overgrown with stunted trees, and you can't see the bottom from this trail.

Turn right at Cam End, and follow Cam Fell High Road north-west. This is a long uphill slog. The trail becomes rough road before it tops out at 577 metres at a place called Kidhow, which is on top of Oughtershaw Side. The view south from here is incredible. Continuing, you eventually reach the top of the Fleet Moss road climb, named after the scary-looking bog next to it. Turn right and descend to Beckermonds, taking care because it's very steep. Go left at the bottom of the hill and head back to Hubberholme.

33 Rosedale Round

A dramatic but very doable ride around one of the dales of the North Yorkshire Moors

DIFFICULTY RATING **7/10** WILDNESS RATING **8/10**

First off, the difficulty rating of this ride depends on doing it in an anti-clockwise direction. Do it clockwise and you have to climb Rosedale Chimney, with its fearsome 33% gradient. Not only that: you would also have to tackle this ramp of rough road straight away. It would boost the ride's difficulty rating to 10/10.

So anti-clockwise it is, because going that way makes this ride exciting and accessible. It's not too long, and it follows the trackbed of an old railway a lot of the way, so the railway engineers have dealt with any steep hills for you.

FACT FILE

Where North Yorkshire Moors, 10 kilometres due north of the A170. Nearest towns are Kirkbymoorside in the west and Pickering in the east

OS grid ref SE 7238 9595

Start/Finish Rosedale Abbey

Ride distance 18.5 kilometres (11.5 miles)

Highest point Blakey Ridge (393 metres). Ten kilometres of this ride are above 300 metres

Approximate time 3–4 hours

Of course, you still have to descend Rosedale Chimney going anti-clockwise, which is a feat of daring and skill in itself. I'll get to that later. And you could always turn around and climb the brute at the end, just because it's there.

From the centre of Rosedale Abbey head north on New Road, then go straight on Daleside Road where New Road, or Bell End Green as it becomes, goes right. This first section is uphill and quite steep in places, but nowhere near Rosedale Chimney-steep. After 2.6 kilometres you reach a row of terraced cottages on either side of the road. Turn right where the left-hand row ends, and follow the lane to a converted railway line. This goes around Upper Rosedale, and you follow it most of the way.

The original railway was built in 1864 by the Rosedale and Ferryhill Iron Company, who mined ironstone deposits in the dale. There were several mine workings in this part of Rosedale, called collectively the Rosedale East Mines. You see the first evidence of them 4 kilometres into the ride.

You'll also see the remains of calcining kilns right beside the trail. The ironstone was processed in these, to purify the iron ore, before being hauled out by steam locomotives to larger railways. It was then carried to the ironworks of Consett and Ferryhill in County Durham. There's an excellent website dedicated to the history of mining in Rosedale, www.rosedalerailway.org.uk, which contains much more information.

Mining ended here in 1926, and peace returned to Rosedale. It's hard to imagine the noise and bustle there was up here, when between 1861 and 1871 the population grew from 461 to 2,048. The cottages you passed climbing up to the old railway were just a few of those built for the miners. A school was built for their children a little further down the dale.

The cuttings you start riding through as you continue north along the track are a terrific feat of engineering. The last is at the dale head, where it's worth stopping to look along the length of Rosedale at its farms and the beautiful River Seven. It rises just above you at Rosedale Head, and passes through a culvert under the railway line to emerge in the valley it formed over millennia.

Similar rivers cut the other dales

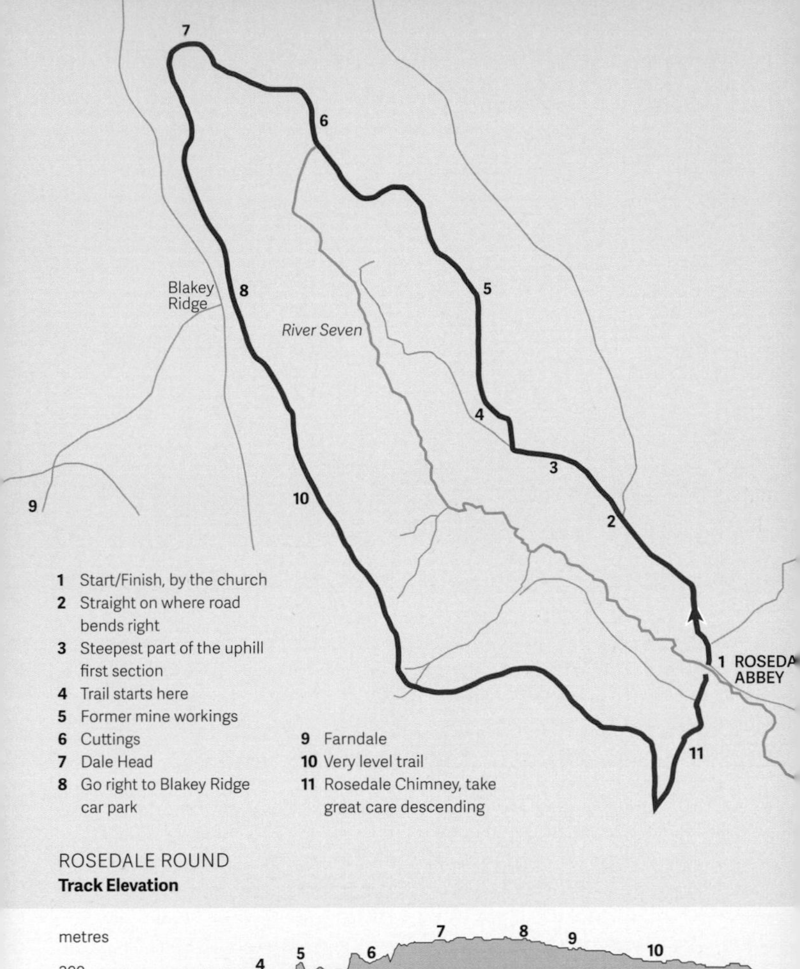

ROSEDALE ROUND

Track Elevation

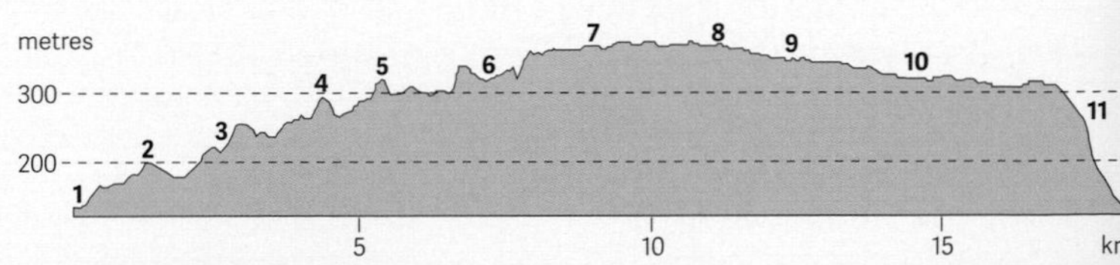

or valleys into the North Yorkshire Moors plateau you see today. You can cross over to another during the next part of this route. Three kilometres after the dale head there are two rough trails going off on your right over an embankment. Pick either of them, ride or walk up and over the embankment, and you are in a car park on Blakey Ridge. Continue through the car park, cross the road, and below you lies Farndale, famous for a wonderful display of wild daffodils each spring.

If you start descending the very steep Blakey Bank road opposite, after 20 metres there's a trail on the right. It's possible to follow this almost all the way around Farndale for another spectacular ride. Adding it to the Rosedale Round would make a rewarding and quite strenuous challenge.

Back in Rosedale, head south. This is a lovely easy stretch, because the trail keeps its altitude by following the contours, so by the time the trail ends at the top of Rosedale Chimney you are 177 metres above the valley floor. You lose all those metres in the rush of the next 1.5 kilometres.

Turn left on the road and get ready. Control your speed over the first 200 metres, because after that the road drops away suddenly. If your bike has dropped handlebars then always hold the bottoms, and brake from that hand position. Brake harder with your rear rather than the front on very steep bits, although you'll need both. It helps to move your weight to the back of the saddle. Really lower your speed before the sharp right and left bends near the bottom. The surface is quite rough after them. Keep these things in mind if you aren't an experienced descender. Even if you are, going down Rosedale Chimney demands respect.

Now all that's left is to turn around and ride back up the hill. Only joking. You're back in Rosedale Abbey where the ride started. Unfortunately, there's no abbey to visit if you were looking forward to that. All that's left is a spiral staircase, a stone pillar and a sundial, where a Cistercian Priory once stood. It was run by nuns who, legend has it, founded sheep farming in this dale during the 12th century. The priory's stone was used in the 19th century to build the church standing on the priory site today.

34 The Cinder Track

A spectacular cycle trail along the North Yorkshire coast

DIFFICULTY RATING **6/10** WILDNESS RATING **7/10**

I haven't included any designated cycleways in their entirety, but this one between Scarborough and Whitby has be in *Wild Cycling*. It's high and wild, but because it follows an old railway line it is high and wild without too many hills. It can be done in one go, but with lots of car parks along the way it can also be chopped into shorter rides. It's ideal for families with younger children, and for less experienced cyclists.

It's called the Cinder Track because locals called it that after Scarborough Council bought the railway line that closed in 1965. Cinders rather than crushed stone were used as ballast for the original track, and the same cinders were used to create the trail, which is part of Route 1 of the National Cycle Network.

I chose Scarborough to start from, but it's equally good from Whitby. The first section undulates north from the middle of Scarborough's North Bay, then goes inland to Newby, where it swings north again for the steady climb up Burniston Beck.

Apart from the odd glimpse between hills the first proper sea view since Scarborough comes after 9 kilometres. You'll play hide-and-seek with the sea for the rest of the ride. There are a number of quiet beaches you could visit along the way: Hayburn Wyke is the first, at 11 kilometres.

Continuing north, the trail gradient, which has been steadily uphill, begins to steepen. Cuttings helped the railway through any extra lumps and bumps in its path, and they help us cyclists now. After a road crossing at 15 kilometres there's a terrific sea view. It's close to the Ravenscar summit of the ride, where the sea is less than

FACT FILE

Where Scarborough is 56 kilometres north-east of York

OS grid ref TA 0369 8973

Start/Finish Scarborough end of the Scarborough-to-Whitby Trail

Ride distance For the trail, 28 kilometres (17.5 miles). To Whitby, 34.4 kilometres (21 miles)

Highest point Ravenscar (195 metres)

Approximate time 3–4 hours

ALEXRIMS

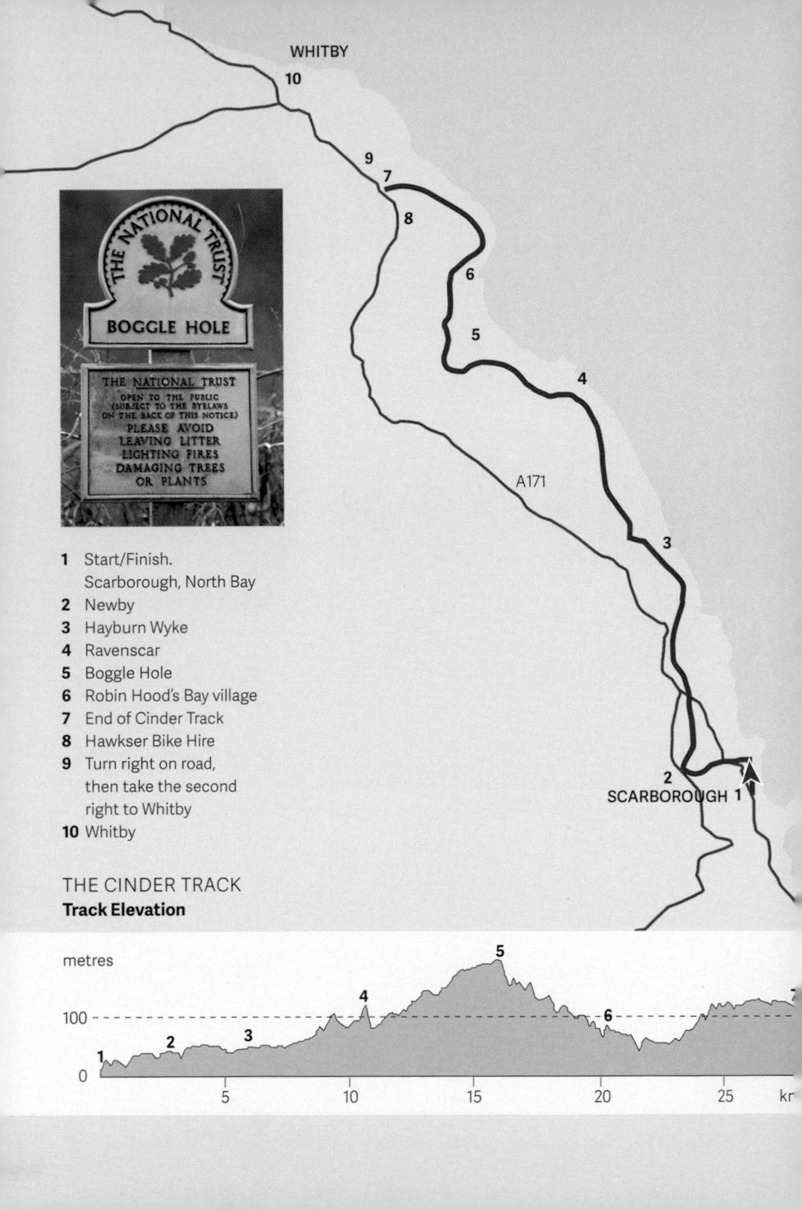
WHITBY
10
9
7
8
6
5
4
A171
3
2
SCARBOROUGH 1
THE NATIONAL TRUST
BOGGLE HOLE
THE NATIONAL TRUST
OPEN TO THE PUBLIC
(SUBJECT TO THE BYELAWS
ON THE BACK OF THIS NOTICE)
PLEASE AVOID
LEAVING LITTER
LIGHTING FIRES
DAMAGING TREES
OR PLANTS
1 Start/Finish. Scarborough, North Bay
2 Newby
3 Hayburn Wyke
4 Ravenscar
5 Boggle Hole
6 Robin Hood's Bay village
7 End of Cinder Track
8 Hawkser Bike Hire
9 Turn right on road, then take the second right to Whitby
10 Whitby
THE CINDER TRACK
Track Elevation
metres
100
0
1
2
3
4
5
6
5
10
15
20
25

Apart from the odd glimpse between hills the first proper sea view since Scarborough comes after 9 kilometres. You'll play hide-and-seek with the sea for the rest of the ride.

500 metres away but 195 metres below you. Cloughton Café in Ravenscar village is a good place to stop.

From Ravenscar the trail traces the shape of Robin Hood's Bay to the village of the same name. This is the best-looking bit of the entire ride. Boggle Hole halfway around the bay has an excellent Youth Hostel. Robin Hood's Bay, the place, is at the northern end of the bay, and the trail goes through the western edge of this gorgeous and largely unspoilt fishing village. The way down to the beach is steep, but it's really worth visiting.

The final section of the trail follows the outline of Ness Point, ending in Hawkser, the trail head, where there's a bike hire place. Go right on the main road, then take the second right, signposted Whitby Abbey. A long straight lane leads to the top of Whitby. With its maritime and literary connections, it's a fascinating town to visit. Best fish and chips in Britain, too.

35 Arkengarth and Swaledale
Sampling the wild sides of the two most northerly Yorkshire Dales

DIFFICULTY RATING **8/10** WILDNESS RATING **8/10**

This ride starts in Swaledale, offers a glimpse into Arkengarthdale, then returns over the windswept tops and ends with an idyllic ride along the swirling Swale, the river named after the Anglo-Saxon word *Sualuae*, meaning rapid and liable to deluge.

There's a lot of wild-cycling potential in Arkengarth and Swaledale, but the high routes can be tricky, so lend themselves to mountain-bike exploration, although a cyclo-cross or gravel bike should do fine for this ride. It only has a few of the really rutted trails, where old lead mining operations have accelerated erosion.

Swaledale starts on the Yorkshire/Cumbria border, and Upper Swaledale is really wild, but there are few roads and bridleways, a sharp contrast to lower down. That's why I chose the lovely stone village of Reeth at the confluence of the River Swale and Arkle Beck to start this ride.

Find the Dales Centre in Reeth – there's also a very interesting Swaledale Museum of Rural Life there – and head north-west on a road that's part of NCN route 71, which links the Yorkshire Dales with the Lake District. It's an uphill start but not too steep, and the views north and west across Arkengarthdale are fabulous.

The 4-kilometre-long Fremington Edge stands out across the dale. It formed after the last Ice Age, when meltwater caused widespread landslip along the northern side of Arkengarthdale, leaving a limestone cliff. The landslip revealed veins of the crystal lead ore galena in the cliffs, and much of the scree below them is waste and rubble from old lead mines. You see lots more evidence of lead mining on this ride, and evidence of the technique used to wash the ore out of the rock, which was quite devastating,

FACT FILE

Where Reeth is 15 kilometres west of Richmond, which is 5 kilometres west of both the Catterick and Scotch Corner exits of the A1

OS grid ref SE 0377 9935

Start/Finish Dales Centre, Reeth

Ride distance 26.3 kilometres (16.4 miles)

Highest point Great Pinseat (575 metres)

Approximate time 3–4 hours

726

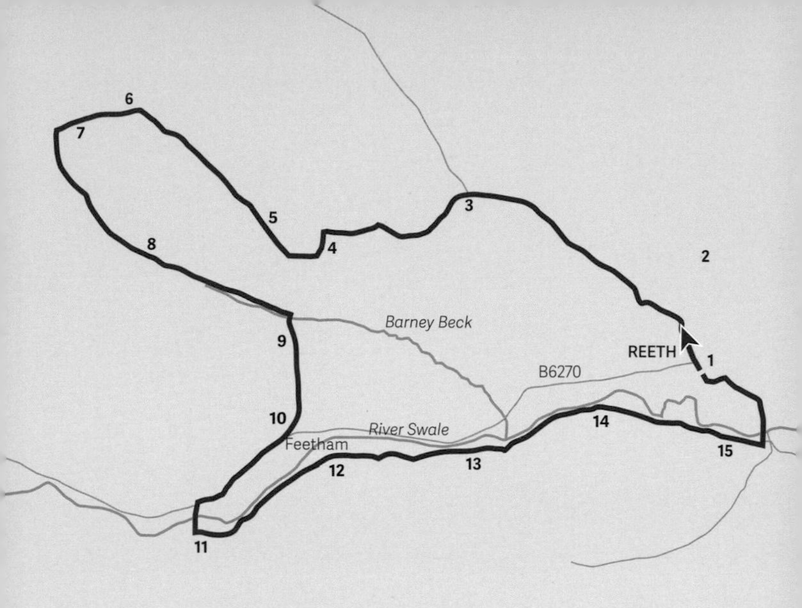

ARKENGARTH AND SWALEDALE

Track Elevation

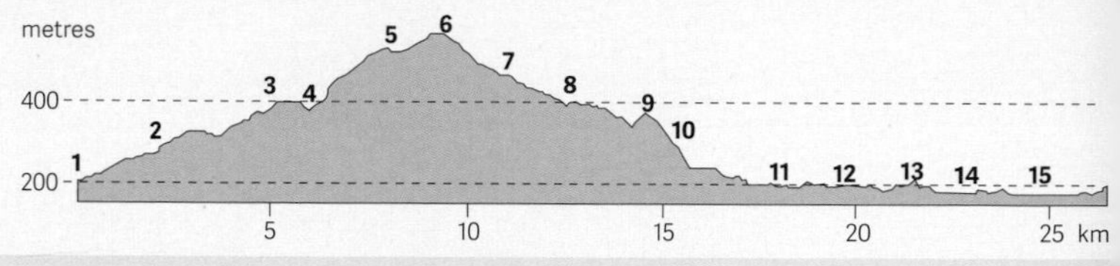

1 Start/Finish
2 Fremington Edge
3 Start of first trail section
4 Ford
5 Long off-road climb
6 Top of Pinseat, lots of erosion
7 Descent rutted, take care
8 Trail cut up near old mine buildings
9 Short uphill
10 Very steep descent
11 Left at phone box
12 Trail
13 Road
14 Trail
15 Road

although nature is slowly healing the scars.

After 3 kilometres, almost all uphill, there's a short descent and a signposted bridleway going off to your left. Follow the bridleway for a kilometre of fairly good but uphill trail across Reeth Low Moor. Then there's a short descent to a road, where you go left and through a ford. There's a footbridge across the stream to use if you like, but it's narrow and you have to carry your bike. Definitely use the footbridge if the stream is flowing fast and deep, which happens after prolonged rain.

Once across the ford, after a further 200 metres of road join the bridleway on your right to begin the 3-kilometre climb up a wide track to the summit of Great Pinseat. It's like the surface of the moon up here, with cratered mounds of light grey limestone waste. It's all the result of mining, and a landscape way past wild – almost alien.

Follow the trail through the old spoil heaps, which is rough and cut up in places, so take care, and you start descending, straight at first, but later swinging left into the valley of Hard Level Gill. Follow the valley down to the road at Mill Bottom. There are lots of old mine buildings and works to examine on the way, plus possibilities to extend the ride on this section. Some of the offshoots from this trail are very broken, but would make adventurous and demanding rides. Something to come back to, maybe?

Turn right on reaching the road, climb a short but steep hill, then descend across Feetham Pasture to Feetham, a descent that gets very steep towards the bottom. Turn right on the B6270, the road that runs along the length of Swaledale, from Kirkby Stephen in Cumbria almost as far as Richmond in North Yorkshire, and head south-west for a kilometre to the first bridge across the Swale. Turn left, cross the bridge, then at a telephone box turn immediately left.

Continue along this road next to the Swale. The road becomes a walled track at some isolated buildings. Carry on east to join another metalled road, still heading east. After a kilometre there's a grassy bridleway on the left: follow this down to the river and alongside it again.

Join a tarmac road at Swale Hall, turn left by the church in Grinton, and follow the B6270 across the Swale, and back into Reeth to complete a great ride that samples the wild-cycling possibilities of Arkengarth and Swaledale.

There are many other routes here: high and low ones, as well as easy and very adventurous rides. The high routes are best done outside of winter, because then the hilltops are regularly covered by snow. Avoid the last week of May and first week of June for this one, because the very busy Swaledale Festival is centred on Reeth. And the annual Reeth Show is held on the final Wednesday of every August.

8

The North-West

36 Kinder Trespass

A tough little loop that celebrates the origins of access to wild places for everyone

DIFFICULTY RATING **8/10** WILDNESS RATING **8/10**

In 1932 Benny Rothman and a group of friends climbed Kinder Scout in the High Peak District. Pretty unremarkable, you might think, but in those days huge areas of the English countryside were closed to walkers. Rothman was a social activist who believed human rights included the right to roam in wild places, even if that meant putting himself in harm's way.

Trespass is not a criminal offence now, but back then the walkers were met by a group of gamekeepers who tried to stop them. The police were there to keep order, and when scuffles broke out Rothman and some of his friends ended up in prison. The incident is known as the Mass Trespass of Kinder Scout, and in time it led to the definition of open country under the 1949 National Parks Act. Vast areas of countryside are open now for all to wander, and to ride, and we owe that to Benny Rothman and friends.

You can't actually ride the trespassers' route, because it's a designated footpath, but there are bridleways close to it, so cyclists can celebrate Rothman and his brave pioneers on two wheels, by doing the route here and other wild rides around this gaunt but striking place.

The Mass Trespass began in Bowden Bridge Quarry near Hayfield, which is a car park today. There's a plaque on the wall commemorating the day. All in all, it's an ideal place to start this ride, an exploration of the south-west High Peak.

The route follows the trespassers' way for only a mile, but it follows their spirit all the way. Go left out of the car park onto a narrow road, then turn right opposite the first building you come to on your left.

FACT FILE

Where Western Peak District, just south-east of Greater Manchester

OS grid ref SK 0472 8688

Start/Finish Bowden Bridge, just east of Hayfield

Ride distance 18 kilometres (11.25 miles)

Highest points Kinderlow End (427 metres), Hills Farm Top (440 metres)

Approximate time 2–4 hours

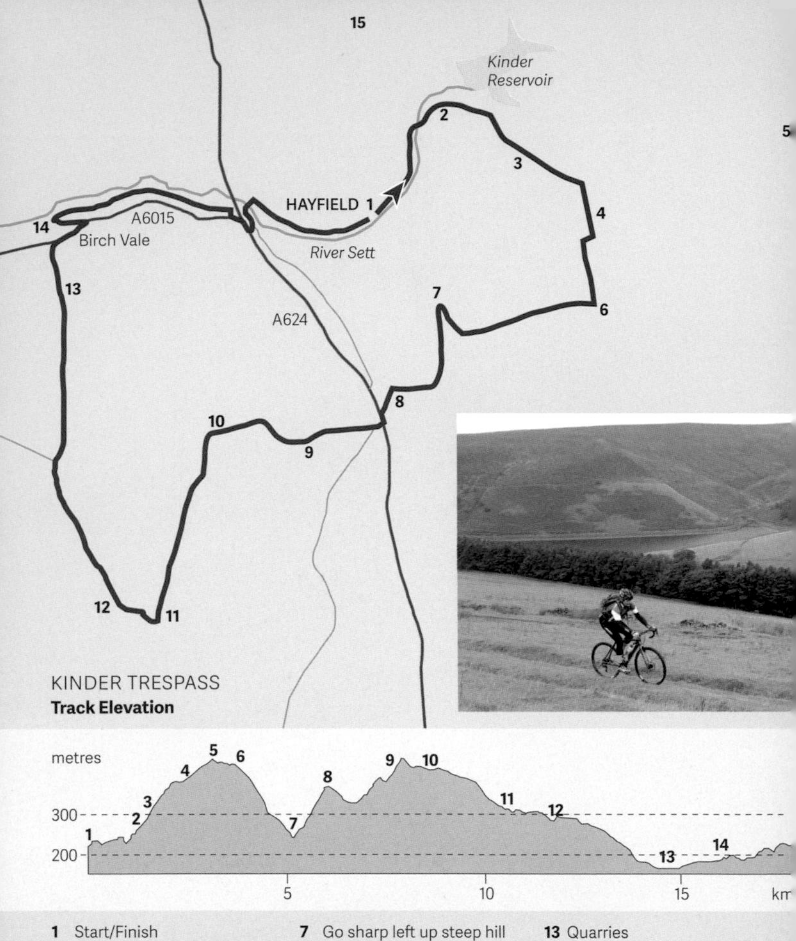

1 Start/Finish
2 Take bridleway on right
3 Hard uphill slog
4 Walled trail
5 Kinder Scout
6 Left here if you want to see the view of Edale, otherwise go right
7 Go sharp left up steep hill
8 Trail crossing then left on road and right off it
9 Long uphill
10 Go right after crossing stream head
11 Steep descent
12 Keep right
13 Quarries
14 Go right to Sett Valley Trail
15 Footpath original trespassers used

The trespassers went left on this road, joining a footpath to climb William Clough and up onto the Kinder Plateau. Bikes take the first bridleway on the right, which climbs Broad Clough.

You can see where the trespassers went, and the craggy-edged top of Kinder Scout. It is an impressive sight: a high, flat table with a ruffled cloth of heather and three hardly detectable summits. The highest, at 636 metres (2,088 feet), is the highest place in the Peak District. Kinder Scout's sides are scarred by craggy gaches, with the amazing Kinder Downfall its hidden jewel.

Broad Clough is a grassy climb, and after you fork right, away from the trees, it's pretty heavy going. Low gears and a mountain bike make this ride easier, but I managed on a cyclo-cross bike. Eventually you turn sharp right to follow a walled trail.

Progress becomes even more difficult where the route flattens around the shoulders of Kinderlow End. Lush, sheep-cropped grass gives way to straggly sedge and soggy peat. The trail is eroded and lumpy here, but you can have great fun whooshing down one mound and trying to gain enough momentum to clear the next.

Eventually you reach Oaken Clough. Clough is a northern name for deep valley. There's a choice here. The route goes right down Oaken Clough for the first descent of the day. Or you could go left, if you don't mind a mile-long ride-cum-walk, because the trail is very rough going. Eventually you get to Edale Cross and can look down into Edale. In anything but the dullest weather the view is magnificent.

This section is a perfect example of how today's bridleways were once important roads. Hayfield to Edale via Oaken Clough is the direct route over the Kinder massif, whereas others, such as Snake Pass, go around it and are many miles longer. This is the way packhorses and traders used to travel. Walking trails like this was how communities kept in touch, and how in rural areas news only ever spread at walking pace.

Whether you choose to have a look at Edale or not, back on this route descending by Oaken Clough requires care. It's better to walk than risk a fall on the sharp rocks. The track eventually joins a good concrete road. This dives into Coldwell Clough, where you take the first bridleway on your left. The trail goes very steeply uphill now: you might need to dismount to push up some of this section.

Go straight at the trail crossroads, then turn left on reaching the A624. After 100 metres take the first right – be careful of traffic – and ride down a farm track to Peep-o-Day Farm. The hardest climb of the day starts here.

It goes up past Hills Farm and over the 430-metre contour. Ignore the

path fork on your left: it's a footpath, so no bikes. The views from the top are breathtaking. Kinder is behind, and in front the tawny moors gently roll down to the green Cheshire Plain. South Manchester is a little to the north, and you are directly under the flightpath of planes descending gracefully into Manchester airport.

Turn left, so south, at the summit, after crossing a spring where the stream flows north, and descend to a road. The descent is quite gentle at first, but gets steeper near the road. Turn right on Over Hill Road, then right where it gets a bit rougher, and keep descending to Birch Vale. Turn right on the A6015 Hayfield Road, then left on Station Road. Where a row of houses on your right ends, you'll see an entrance for the Sett Valley Trail. Turn right and head towards Hayfield.

Once there, you have to cross the A624. Turn right at the end of the trail on Station Road. Go left on the A6015, turn left to the A624 junction and, when it's clear, cross and go right to the cycle lane on the far carriageway. Turn first left onto Church Street, go past St Matthew's Church, and go right on Bank Street and right onto Kinder Road. This takes you back to the start. Look out for the blue plaque on the wall of one of the terraced houses on your left. It's the birthplace of the actor, Arthur Lowe, who was Captain Mainwaring in *Dad's Army*.

37 Rivington and Anglezarke
Around the reservoirs and hills of the West Pennine Moors

DIFFICULTY RATING **7/10** WILDNESS RATING **7/10**

This ride is in a little piece of cycling heaven tucked between the densely populated towns north of Manchester. The 2002 Commonwealth Games road race was held in this area, while the mountain-bike races were up on the witchy heights above where this ride starts, at Rivington Barn.

Manchester is the home of British Cycling, so lots of famous cyclists train around here. Six-time Olympic gold medallist Jason Kenny comes from nearby Bolton, and although he's a track sprinter he loves clocking up some road miles here. Britain's most successful Olympian of all time, and the country's first Tour de France winner, Sir Bradley Wiggins, is another. In 2015, when he was a Christmas guest editor of BBC Radio 4's *Today* programme, Wiggins told listeners that Rivington Pike was his favourite place to ride. We'll see why later.

As well as hills, moors and wooded valleys, this area has some glorious expanses of water, with the Upper and Lower Rivington, the wonderfully named Anglezarke, and the Yarrow reservoirs. They were all constructed during the second half of the 19th century to provide clean water for Liverpool. Some of the flatter roads and bridleways around the reservoir banks would make perfect family rides, as you'll see soon after setting off.

Head west from Rivington Barn, through the car park and down to the edge of Lower Rivington Reservoir. Turn right, and ride along the bank until you reach Horrobin Lane, opposite Rivington Bowling Club.

There aren't many finer places to stop for a refreshing brew than the bowling club's café, the Tea Room. Inside is basic but homely, while outside it's lovely: seats and tables

FACT FILE

Where Just north of Horwich, junction 6 of the M61

OS grid ref SD 6286 1385

Start/Finish Rivington Barn

Ride distance 23 kilometres (14.4 miles)

Highest points Side of Winter Hill (336 metres), Rivington Pike (343 metres)

Approximate time 3–4 hours

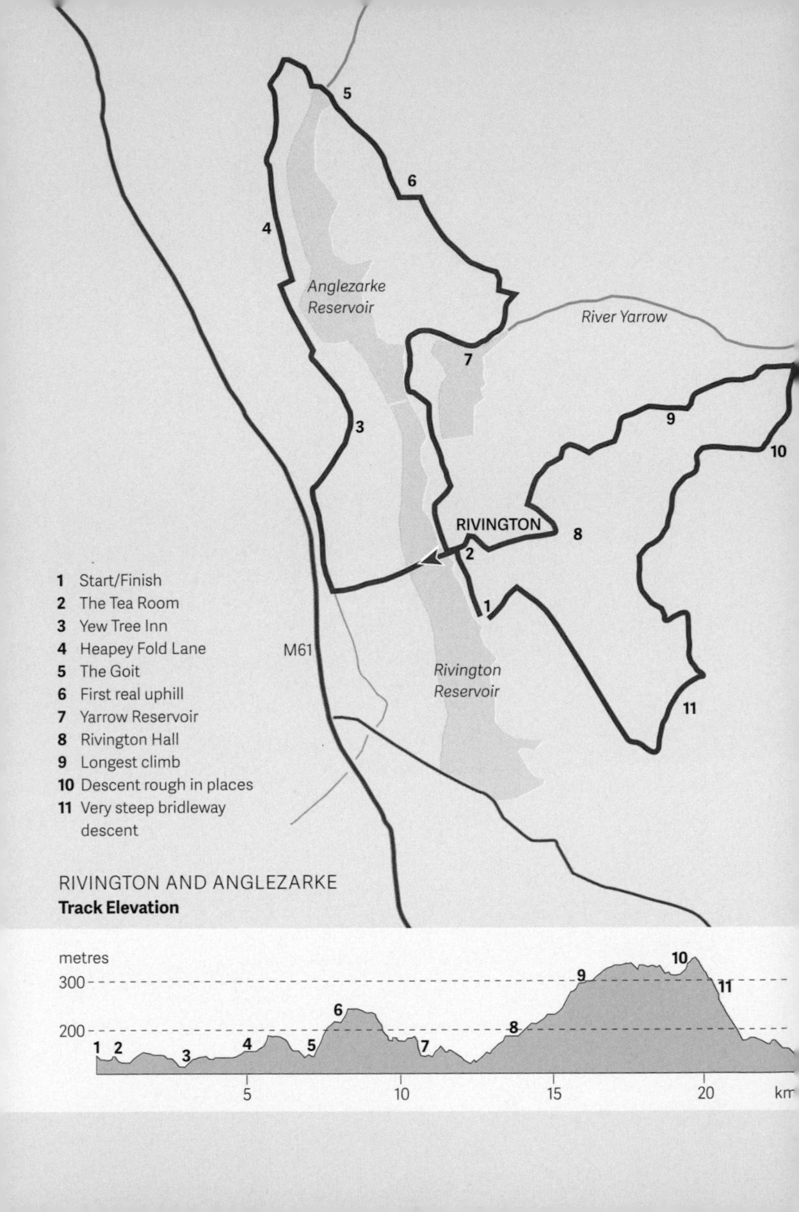

5
6
4
Anglezarke Reservoir
River Yarrow
7
9
3
10
RIVINGTON
8
2
1
M61
Rivington Reservoir
11
1 Start/Finish
2 The Tea Room
3 Yew Tree Inn
4 Heapey Fold Lane
5 The Goit
6 First real uphill
7 Yarrow Reservoir
8 Rivington Hall
9 Longest climb
10 Descent rough in places
11 Very steep bridleway descent
RIVINGTON AND ANGLEZARKE
Track Elevation
metres
300
200
5
10
15
20
km

around a pristine bowling green, and a wonderful outlook across the reservoirs, framed by tall trees. Sitting here in dappled summer sunlight, sipping tea and enjoying a piece of homemade cake, is a joy, but it's too early to stop. Anyway, the ride passes the Tea Room later. There's also a good café at Rivington Barn, so let's press on.

Turn left on Horrobin Lane, then right just before the M61 on New Road, and follow it when it becomes Nickleton Brow and descends to the Yew Tree Inn. Go left on Back Lane, then turn right on the bridleway to Kays Farm, and left at the farm along Heapey Fold Lane. This runs north, parallel to the west bank of Anglezarke Reservoir. Continue north where the lane becomes bridleway and you reach Moor Road, just short of a village called White Coppice. The Noble Prize-winning chemist Walter Haworth, who discovered vitamin C, was born in White Coppice.

Turn right on Moor Road, crossing a small channel called the Goit. Goits are man-made, and are used to collect and channel water from various streams. This Goit channels excess water running off the surrounding moors into Anglezarke Reservoir.

Rivington Reservoirs are fed by excess water from Anglezarke Reservoir, and by the River Yarrow through Yarrow Reservoir. The River Yarrow is interesting: it continues on the other side of Rivington Reservoir, where a huge pump helps it on its way. It then flows under the Leeds and Liverpool Canal, and eventually to the River Douglas and out to sea through the Ribble Estuary.

But enough of rivers. After crossing the Goit, Moor Road climbs towards the second phase of this ride in the West Pennine Moors. They provide a gorgeous backdrop for most of this ride, and offer cyclists challenging terrain, great places to explore, and fantastic views. The moors are called Rivington, Anglezarke and Withnall, and they are bordered on the west by the M61 and on the east by the A675.

Quiet lanes weave around the woods and valleys along the edges of the moors, and a spectacular road goes across them from Rivington to Belmont. Winter Hill is the highest spot on the moors at 456 metres, while the most evocative name here, Anglezarke, is a fascinating lesson in how place names evolve.

It was originally Anlaferg, combining the Norse name Anlaf and the Norse word for pasture, *erg*, so it denoted Anlaf's pasture. By 1202 Anlaferg had become Andelevesarewe, by 1225 it was Anlavesargh, by 1351 it was Anlasargh, and in 1559 it was Anlazarghe, before emerging after that as Anglezarke.

Keep climbing past tiny High Bullough Reservoir, and where Moor Road goes sharp right continue straight on the bridleway. This descends through a couple of zig-zags into Lead Mines Clough. Follow this valley down to Parson's Bullough Road. Continue on the road, and go left on Knowsley Lane until a 90-degree right bend. Go left there on a bridleway that descends to Yarrow Reservoir, then runs alongside it to Rivington Lane, next to Rivington Bowling Club and the Tea Room.

Turn left and follow Horrobin Lane, then right on Rivington Lane through Rivington village, then go left onto the bridleway to Rivington Hall Barn. Turn left at the barn on Hall Lane, then right onto Sheep House Lane. This is the start of a long road climb to the pass between Anglezarke Moor and Winter Hill, where various masts have transmitted TV signals since 1956.

Turn right onto Belmont Road after a kilometre of climbing, then right onto Rivington Road, which wriggles upwards to the pass. However, just when you can see the top, turn right onto Belmont Road and descend. This is an old road; the surface is good

at first, but varies as you descend. Eventually you go left onto a bridleway that climbs to Rivington Pike Tower. The Rivington Pike fell race from Horwich up to here and back, one of the oldest running races in the UK, has been held on Easter Sunday since 1892.

There are two ways around the tower, but the left-hand fork is most fun because of its switchback descent. Cross Belmont Road to a bridleway that is a long steep descent. You can go right on Belmont Road if you don't fancy the steep bridleway descent, and it is probably best suited to mountain bikes, then go left on Roynton Road, then right on Rivington Lane, and follow it back to Rivington Barn.

If you pick the steep way, after 100 metres there's a gate to negotiate, then the trail becomes progressively rutted, and requires care and a bit of skill in places. Keep your speed inside your comfort zone with judicious braking. At the bottom of the descent, go left on Roynton Road, then right on Rivington Road, and head back to Rivington Barn.

38 A Taste of Bowland

A short ride to do any time, that shows the excellent wild cycling the fells of Bowland have to offer

DIFFICULTY RATING **7/10** WILDNESS RATING **7/10**

Bowland is the pride of Lancashire cycling. Properly the area is called the Bowland Fells or Forest of Bowland, which harks back to when named forests, like the New Forest, denoted royal hunting grounds rather than thick tree coverage. The blanket bog on the Bowland fell tops probably never supported trees in human times.

Fell tops, and the conditions on them, are why I have made this a taster ride. It's short, goes up a valley, visits a pass between two tops, then returns down the same valley. There are higher routes and bridleways all over the Bowland Fells, but they are for summer rides in fine weather. The higher bridleways here aren't good for cycling in wet weather or the colder months, but they are splendid when dry.

Having said that, this ride is still wild. It's almost all off-road, shows Bowland's further wild-cycling potential, and starts in Dunsop Bridge, where in 1992 the 100,000th payphone installed in Britain was unveiled by Sir Ranulph Fiennes. They don't come much wilder than Sir Ran.

Head west out of the car park and cross the bridge over the River Dunsop, then turn right after the sharp left and right bends. This section soon changes to trail as you continue alongside the vivacious River Dunsop.

After 3.5 kilometres you reach the confluence of the Brennand River and the Dunsop. Follow the left-hand branch, the Brennand, but on the other side of it. So cross the first of two bridges and go immediately left. Do not cross the second bridge.

Keep left at all trail junctions as you climb the valley to Brennand Farm. Follow the bridleway through the farm, cross another bridge, and

FACT FILE

Where Bowland is just east of the M6 between Preston and Lancaster

OS grid ref SD 6613 5017

Start/Finish Dunsop Bridge

Ride distance 13.3 kilometres (8.3 miles)

Highest points Middle Knoll Pass (309 metres)

Approximate time 1.5 to 2.5 hours

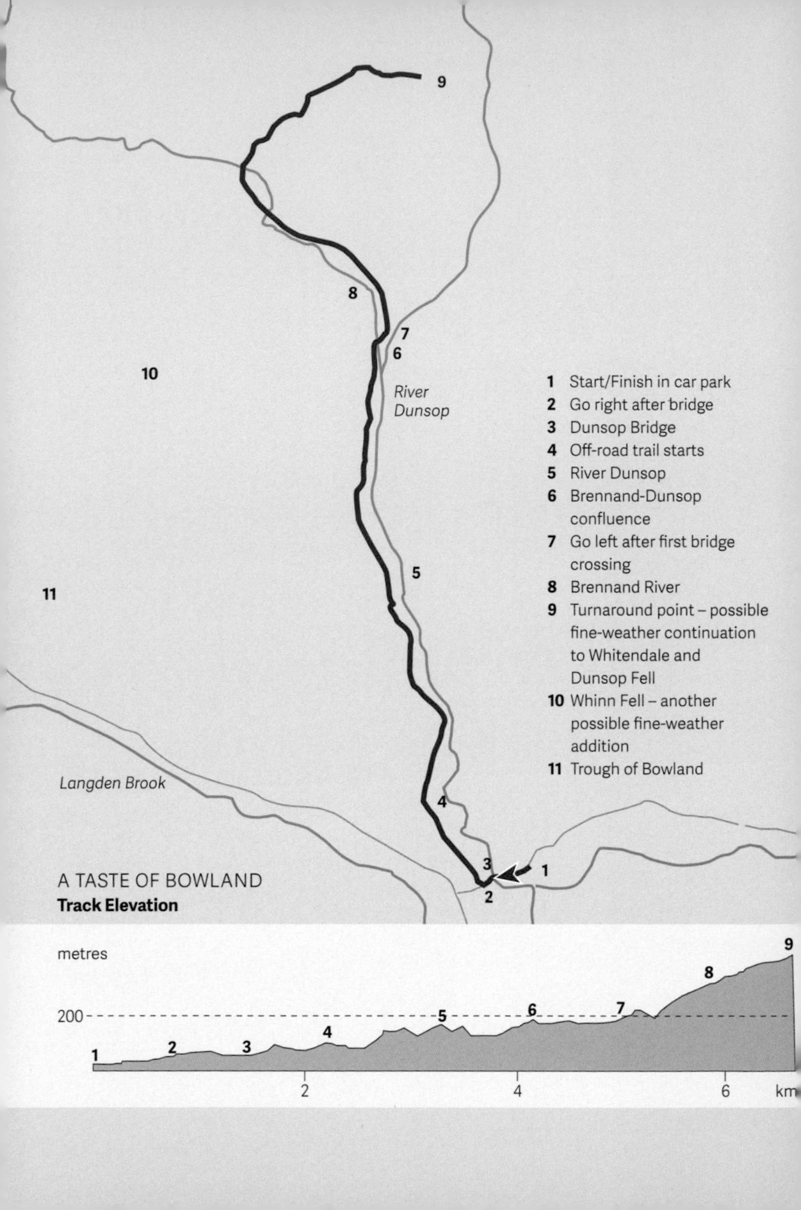
9
8
7
6
10
River
Dunsop
5
11
Langden Brook
4
3
1
2
1 Start/Finish in car park
2 Go right after bridge
3 Dunsop Bridge
4 Off-road trail starts
5 River Dunsop
6 Brennand-Dunsop confluence
7 Go left after first bridge crossing
8 Brennand River
9 Turnaround point – possible fine-weather continuation to Whitendale and Dunsop Fell
10 Whinn Fell – another possible fine-weather addition
11 Trough of Bowland
A TASTE OF BOWLAND
Track Elevation
metres
200
1
2
3
4
5
6
7
8
9
2
4
6
km

continue straight on a trail that heads over the pass between Windy Knoll and Brennand Fell. Ride to the summit of the pass, then turn around and retrace your outward journey back to Dunsop Bridge.

In dry conditions it's possible to continue over the pass this ride turns around on, descend very steeply to Whitendale and continue east to explore Dunsop Fell. Or from Brennand Farm there's a bridleway south-west going over Whinn Fell, then west down Rams Clough to join the Trough of Bowland road. Further north, meanwhile, there's a trail over Croasdale and Salter Fells that is incredible to ride. But these options are for good conditions, riding a cyclo-cross or mountain bike, and for experienced off-road riders.

Properly the area is called the Bowland Fells or Forest of Bowland, which harks back to when named forests, like the New Forest, denoted royal hunting grounds rather than thick tree coverage.

39 A Touch of Fell Magic
An example of Lake District wild-cycling potential

DIFFICULTY RATING **8/10** WILDNESS RATING **8/10**

This is the first of two rides in the Lake District, and they are both quite short, which doesn't mean this glorious place has few wild-cycling opportunities. Quite the opposite: the Lake District has hundreds of incredible high-level trails, but they are demanding and require experience and a good level of fitness. Even this ride, with a long climb up the side of a fell, then a steep and bumpy descent, demands fitness and some experience and skill. It makes a good first-time Lake District high-level ride for anyone who is ready, or could serve as the springboard for further adventure.

Experienced off-road riders could use a cyclo-cross or gravel bike, but a mountain bike is better for this ride. The lakeside trails are undemanding, but the big climb and descent are tough on body and bike alike.

Start at the Cow Bridge car park near Hartsop, and go north on the A592 to Patterdale village, then right across the bridge to Rooking.

To show how much wild cycling there is here, if you were to continue through Patterdale for 500 metres, and turn left at Grisedale Bridge, there is an incredible bridleway route climbing through a gap in the Helvellyn Range to 583 metres at Grisedale Tarn.

Back with this one, go left in Rooking, and follow the bridleway that runs along the south shore of Ullswater to Sandwick. Go right in Sandwick, and keep right to begin climbing up Boredale. Alternatively, you could go straight from Sandwick to Martindale, then right up the much steeper Bannerdale climb for a harder, longer, wild ride.

Go right where the road ends in Boredale, and a bridleway continues up to Boredale Hause, hause being the Lake District word for a mountain

FACT FILE

Where The ride starts 23 kilometres south-west of Penrith and junction 40 of the M6

OS grid ref NY 4035 1316

Start/Finish Cow Green Bridge car park

Ride distance 17 kilometres (10.6 miles)

Highest point Boredale Hause (382 metres)

Approximate time 2–3 hours

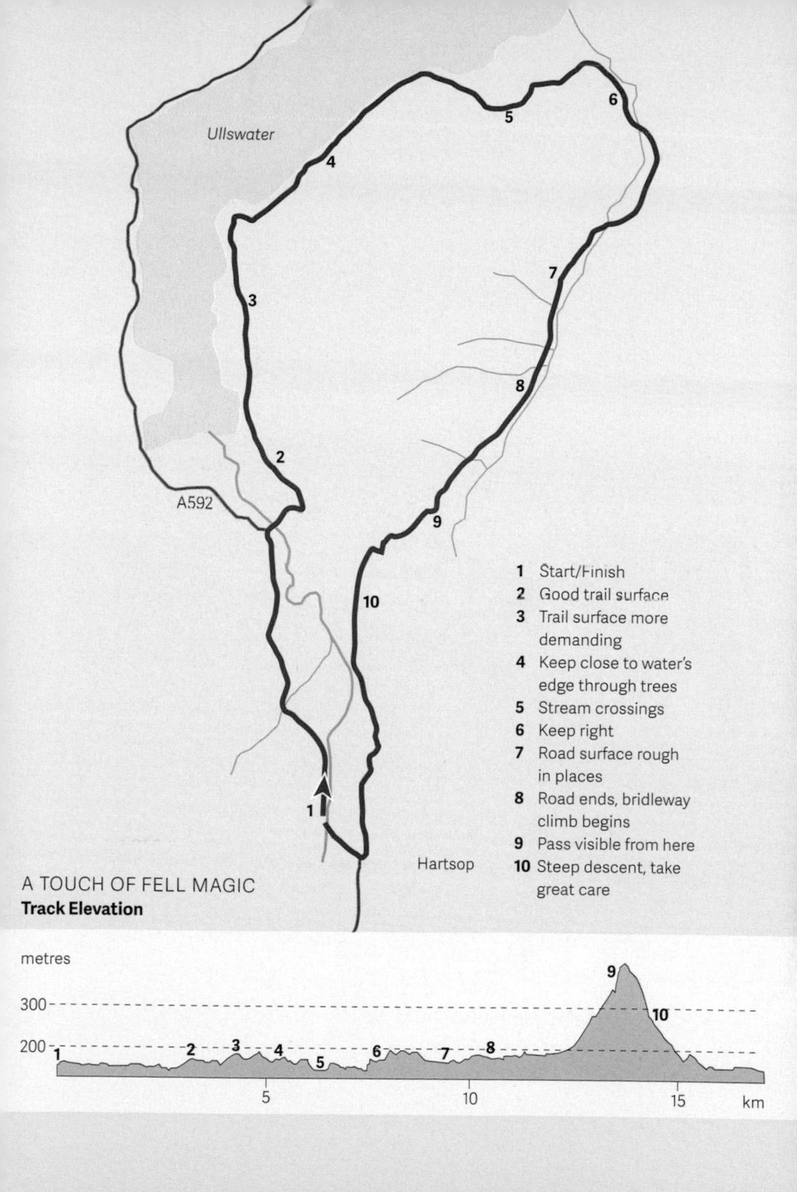
Ullswater
A592
Hartsop
1 Start/Finish
2 Good trail surface
3 Trail surface more demanding
4 Keep close to water's edge through trees
5 Stream crossings
6 Keep right
7 Road surface rough in places
8 Road ends, bridleway climb begins
9 Pass visible from here
10 Steep descent, take great care
A TOUCH OF FELL MAGIC
Track Elevation
metres
300
200
5
10
15
km

The lakeside trails are undemanding, but the big climb and descent are tough on body and bike alike.

pass. The tougher Bannerdale climb also end up here at 380 metres. There is a choice of trails to descend into Patterdale: take the left one going due south, and follow it to the bridge over Goldrill Beck.

This descent is steep, but if you aren't comfortable descending it's only a kilometre to walk down. It's rough in places too, OK for a mountain bike with suspension, but going down on any other bike requires experience and skill, or walking. Once at the bottom, continue on the trail, past the bridge to the Hartsop road, where you turn right and head back to Cow Bridge car park.

Coincidentally, just to underline again the Lake District's wild-cycling potential, if you went left to Hartsop, then right in the village, you'd hit a bridleway that climbs Hayeswater Gill and joins the High Street bridleway. That's an amazing 25-kilometre, high-level, off-road route from near Penrith to Windermere. Put it on your wild-cycling bucket list.

40 Ennerdale Energizer

A straightforward out-and-back ride in a stunning setting that gets tougher towards the turnaround point

DIFFICULTY RATING **6/10** WILDNESS RATING **8/10**

Ennerdale is a jewel of the English Lake District. Its lake, Ennerdale Water, is at the centre of the great Lakeland guidebook writer Alfred Wainwright's Western Fells: a long, deep body of water, oriented roughly east-to-west, open at one end towards the Cumbrian coast, and surrounded by many of the highest Cumbrian mountains at the other.

Ennerdale Water and its valley are glorious. Less visited than other lakes, Ennerdale's deep waters have majesty, its forested sides add mystery, and the surrounding mountains look spectacular. This is the perfect ride to experience Ennerdale: the first part isn't too demanding, but the 2 kilometres to the turnaround are tough. Its wildness factor, although already high at the start, increases as you go.

Start in the Bowness Knott car park, which is named after the almost conical 333-metre peak standing next to it. The car park isn't big, so it might be better to do this ride on a weekday if possible. There are car parking opportunities in Ennerdale Bridge a couple of kilometres to the west as well.

Saddle up and head east: that's basically it for directions on this one. Once out of the car park the trail follows the shore of Ennerdale Water. It has a hard surface at first, with looser and rougher stuff coming nearer the turnaround. Nowhere is the trail super-technical, though.

Ennerdale Water is not a still lake: water flows through it. The River Liza flows into its eastern end, and from there you follow the Liza upstream, always to the north of it. Trails on the south bank are mostly footpaths. Where the river enters Ennerdale Water it's called Charr Dub, named after a fish, the Arctic charr. Charr only live in the coldest waters, so in

FACT FILE

Where Ennerdale is 14 kilometres due east of Whitehaven in Cumbria

OS grid ref NY 1087 1571

Start/Finish Bowness Knott car park

Ride distance 20 kilometres (12.5 miles)

Highest point Black Sail Hut (300 metres)

Approximate time 2–3 hours

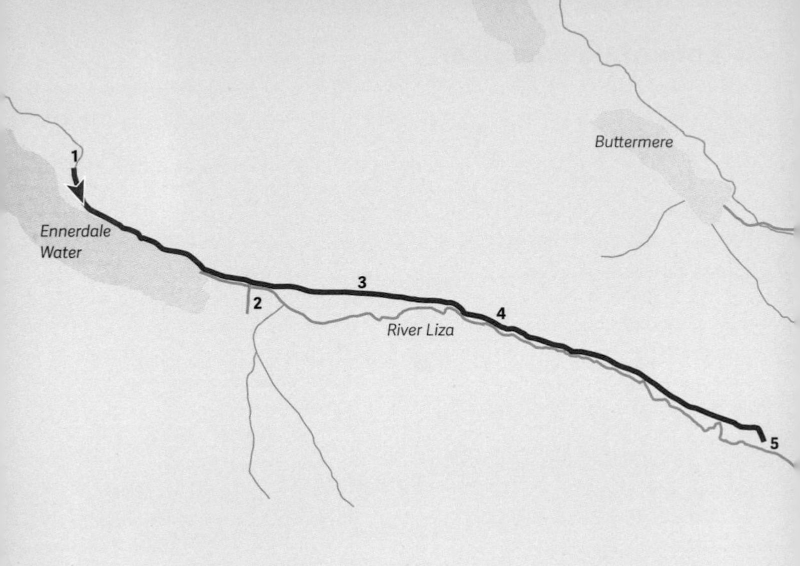

ENNERDALE ENERGIZER

Track Elevation

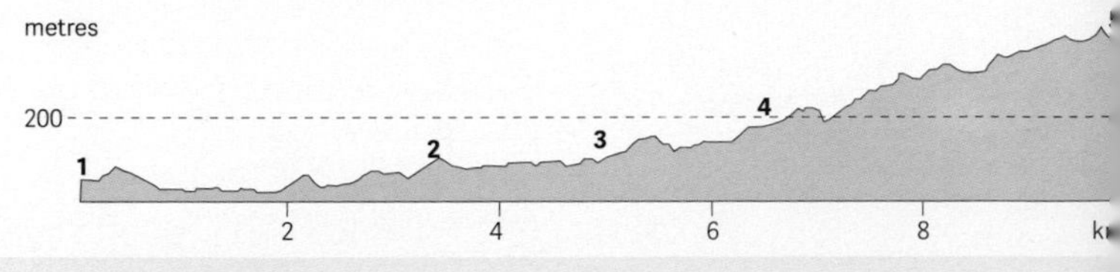

1 Start/Finish
2 Bridge over River Liza
3 Undulating trail
4 Trail begins climbing here
5 Black Sail Hut turnaround

Keep following the trail to Black Sail Hut, a former shepherd's bothy which nowadays is one of the most delightfully isolated Youth Hotels in the country.

---

the UK they are confined to Ennerdale and some of the deepest Scottish lochs. If you go onto the bridge and look down you might see some charr. They are a bit like trout.

Back on the trail it undulates steadily upwards as it follows the Liza, which can vary in size from a trickle to a raging torrent, depending on local rainfall. Keep following the trail to Black Sail Hut, a former shepherd's bothy which nowadays is one of the most delightfully isolated Youth Hotels in the country. The hostel is at the foot of Black Sail Pass, which is the route over into Wasdale. That's a bridleway too, but you'd need to be some athlete to cycle it. For this ride, turn around and retrace your outward journey. Take care going down the steeper first section.

9

The North-East

41 Durham Dales

From Weardale to Waskerley, valley to hill tops using old rail- and roadways

DIFFICULTY RATING **8/10** WILDNESS RATING **8/10**

This ride climbs out of a deep valley, crosses a wild, windy fell top, then plunges back into the valley before following an old mining road home. It's set in the Durham Dales, part of the sparsely populated and statuesque North Pennines, a land of open moors, big skies and muscular hills.

Start in Rookhope, a village built on a high tributary of the River Wear by money made by lead and fluorspar mining. Fluorspar is a crystal found in limestone, and has decorative and practical uses. The poet of limestone regions like this, W. H. Auden, visited Rookhope at the age of 12 and later wrote, 'In Rookhope I was first aware of self and not self, death and dread.' He was a serious kid.

From the Rookhope Inn on the main road go due north off Front Street onto a little lane. Continue past a row of cottages, then go left onto a trail where the lane turns sharp right. You have 1,300 metres of steep climbing now, but the further up you go the better the views get, and the trail surface is quite good. It's part of Sustrans route 7, which goes from Sunderland to Inverness, as well as making up two-thirds of the C2C, coast-to-coast, route.

With the first ascent behind you the trail passes Bolt's Law hilltop, and continues around the edge of a deep valley. It's glorious up here in clear weather, but taxing when the thick mist comes down, so keep an eye on the weather forecast before undertaking this ride.

Eventually you reach a road. You could go right here, descend to Stanhope and get back to the start if the weather turns nasty. Otherwise, turn left, then go right on the next road for a long downhill section. Look out for Smiddy Shaw Reservoir on

FACT FILE

Where Rookhope is 30 kilometres due west of the city of Durham

OS grid ref NY 9389 4292

Start/Finish The Rookhope Inn

Ride distance 32 kilometres (20 miles)

Highest points Top of first climb (518 metres), Rookhope Moor (414 metres)

Approximate time 4–5 hours

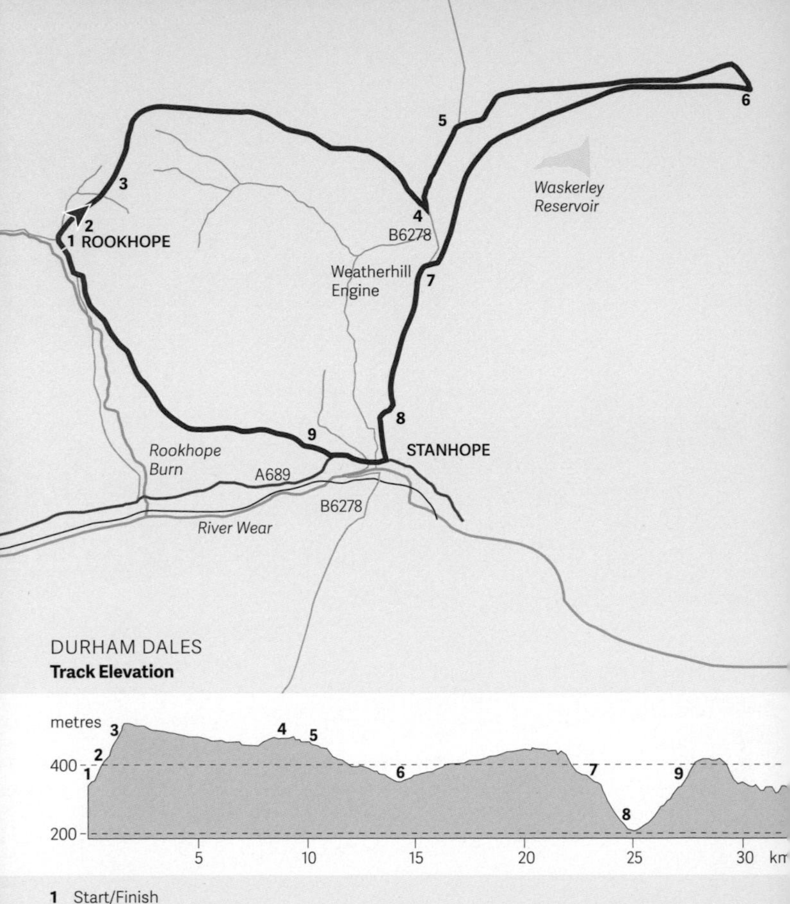

1. Start/Finish
2. Left on trail after cottages
3. Very steep hill
4. Left onto road
5. Right on second road
6. Start of second trail section – go west
7. Left onto road
8. Steep downhill – Crawleyside bends
9. Long climb up narrow lane

The poet of limestone regions like this, W. H. Auden, visited Rookhope at the age of 12 and later wrote, 'In Rookhope I was first aware of self and not self, death and dread'. He was a serious kid.

your left. You need to turn right just after the entrance to the reservoir and ride up the short drag to Waskerley. Here you pick up the C2C trail again, which follows a disused railway line, going west this time, for the next section of the ride.

Turn right onto the trail and head up a long, steady incline, past Waskerley Reservoir, to the site of the Weatherhill Engine. This was used during the early 19th century to haul lime from kilns in Weardale to be loaded on the railway for onward transportation.

Turn left on the road and descend to Stanhope, taking great care through the very steep Crawleyside bends near the bottom. Turn right onto the A689 Wear Valley road, then after a kilometre go right at the caravan park to follow a former mine road over the edges of Rookhope Moor and back into Rookhope.

42 The Coal Round

A circuit of the regenerated West Durham coalfield and its industrial heritage

DIFFICULTY RATING **6/10** WILDNESS RATING **6/10**

It's amazing how much the Durham coalfield has changed. There used to be hundreds of mines, either hillside drifts or deep collieries, along this ride, and they are all long gone. The buildings have been removed, the spoil heaps reclaimed, but some of the heritage has been preserved, particularly in a place close to where the ride starts: the Beamish Open Air Museum.

Beamish does a fantastic job presenting what urban and rural life was like around here at the height of industrialisation, during the first half of the 20th century. There's a town, a railway, a colliery village and lots of other exhibits. Many are original buildings that have been relocated and rebuilt on the museum site. It really is worth visiting, if only for Davey's Fried Fish and Chip Potato Restaurant, which does fish and chips in the way they used to be done, fried in beef dripping on a coal range. Sounds terrible, but tastes delicious, and one helping won't hurt you.

The start of this ride is not at the museum, but rather a small car park just off the road that leads down to it from the A693. The car park is close to the C2C cycle trail, and the ride uses two converted railway lines that are part of the National Cycle Network.

From the car park there's a narrow trail going west out into some woods. After 100 metres there's a short path that goes left to the C2C trail. Follow this, then turn right onto the trail, and continue on it through the north of Stanley. You'll find the C2C quite easy to follow; it's marked out very clearly.

Next up is a place that could be of interest to American visitors. It's Oxhill, a tiny settlement apparently named after its pub, the Ox. Oxhill's claim to

FACT FILE

Where Beamish is 8 kilometres west of junction 63, Chester-le-Street, on the A1(M)

OS grid ref NZ 2194 5373

Start/Finish Car park on the road from the A693 to Beamish Museum

Ride distance 40 kilometres (25 miles)

Highest point C2C trail south of Consett (266 metres)

Approximate time 3.5 to 4.5 hours

American fame is that it's the birthplace of Hugh Rodham, grandfather of the former First Lady, then Presidential candidate, Hillary Clinton. Hugh was the son of a miner, Jonathan Rodham, who emigrated to Pennsylvania in 1883 when Hugh was four.

Continuing along the C2C, approaching Consett, you reach the Jolly Drovers Maze, a circular maze designed by the north-country sculptor and specialist in land art, Andy Goldsworthy. It's built on the site of the Eden Pit Colliery, and the C2C plays with the edges of the maze by going through it in a series of bends. They'll appeal to your inner child as you slalom along.

The Consett section is where you change trails from the C2C to route 14, which zig-zags cross-country from Darlington to South Shields. The trail switch happens just before Hownsgill Viaduct crosses a quite deep but narrow valley. You go north on route 14 across open land at first, then across the A692 and a couple of other roads in the Blackhill area of Consett. Watch out for the trail bollards and half-gates at trail entrances. At some road crossings they are straight across the street; at others they are staggered.

Consett grew from a small settlement into a town because of

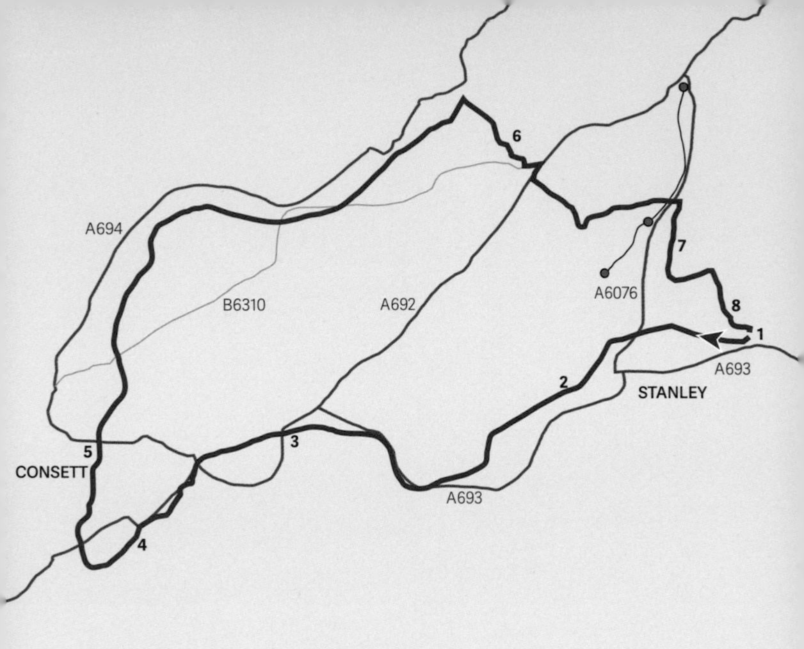

THE COAL ROUND

Track Elevation

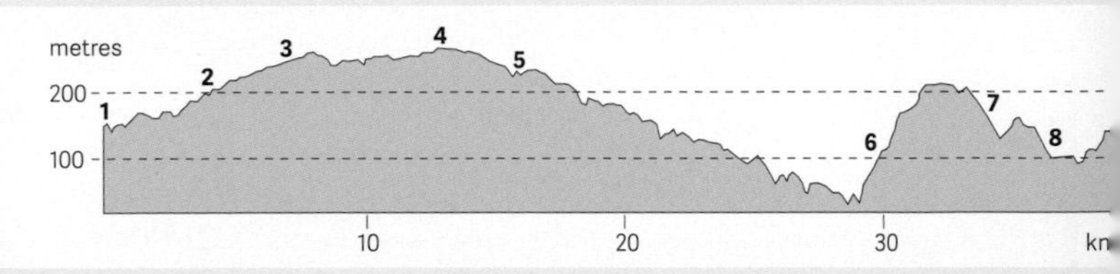

1 Start/Finish
2 Oxhill
3 Jolly Drovers Maze
4 Highest point of ride
5 Careful at the road crossings
6 Steep uphill
7 Steep downhill
8 Beamish Museum

its iron and steel works. These were founded in 1864 to exploit locally quarried iron ore and coke from the Durham coalfield. Consett steel was used to build Blackpool tower and many other structures, but the plant closed in 1980. The reason given was rationalisation, and the consequence was getting on for 4,000 direct job losses, and probably as many again in ancillary businesses. There was no way the local jobs market could absorb redundancy on this scale, and in the early 1980s unemployment in Consett was running at over 30 per cent. The town is still recovering.

The ride continues through Shotley Bridge, which has a much older connection with iron and steel. This is where a group of German sword makers fled in 1691 to escape religious persecution. With local iron deposits and the fast-flowing River Derwent to power their rudimentary tools, they had all they needed to continue their craft.

The trail follows the course of the Derwent now, past the valley-side villages of Ebchester and Hamsterley. The latter is not to be confused with another Hamsterley a little further south from here, and its mountain-bike Mecca of Hamsterley Forest.

Eventually you cross two tributaries, then the Derwent itself, on viaducts, to reach Stirling Lane in Rowland's Gill. Turn right, then go almost immediately right again onto Burnopfield Road, and start climbing Busty Bank.

Take the left fork where the road splits halfway up to join the B6310. Turn left, then after 500 metres sharp right onto the A692 for a further 300 metres, and go left on Barcusclose Lane. Turn left at the next T-junction, cross the A6076, and go right on Beamish Burn Road. Follow this downhill to just before the bridge over Beamish Burn, and turn left past Beamish Hall and through the Beamish Museum site to where you started.

43 Secret Valley and Splendid Quay

A ride through the history and architecture that make Newcastle upon Tyne a jewel of the north-east

DIFFICULTY RATING **3/10** WILDNESS RATING **4/10**

This ride, shaped like a wobbly lop-sided anchor, goes from Gosforth south through Newcastle upon Tyne's secret valley, then west along the River Tyne's famous Quayside, and east to the end of Hadrian's Wall before returning to Gosforth. While doing so it explores some of the history, regeneration and culture of this great northern city.

Start in Gosforth at the northern end of Jesmond Dene, the 'secret valley' that is a slash of green space running from Newcastle's northern suburbs right into the heart of the city. It's a gorge formed by the Ouseburn River, and was owned, developed and then given to the city by William George Armstrong, founder of the great Armstrong-Whitworth shipbuilding and engineering business. The city council owns Jesmond Dene now, and there's a footpath and a cycleway for most of its length. It's a delight: quiet, shady and with no real hills.

There is plenty of street parking in Gosforth. Find the South Gosforth Metro station and ride east on Station Road until you see the Jesmond Dene signs. Head south on the Dene cycleway. Soon there's a section through suburban streets, but clear cycleway signs take you through it. Once back in Jesmond Dene continue south through Armstrong Park and Heaton Park.

A road section comes next, but cycleway signs continue, and after a few quiet streets and traffic-free roads you pass under the railway viaduct into Byker, the first real clue that you are cycling through a city. Byker is famous for the TV series *Byker Grove*, and *Ant and Dec*, but also for the award-winning Byker Wall block of flats, acclaimed when built for its

FACT FILE

Where Newcastle upon Tyne

OS grid ref NZ 2522 6783

Start/Finish South Gosforth, near the Metro station

Ride distance 27.5 kilometres (17.2 miles)

Highest point The start and finish (61 metres)

Approximate time 2 hours, but sightseeing could make it a lot longer

'innovative and visionary design'. The route gets a bit complicated now, but is still clearly marked.

This area used to be full of glass factories, but now has a growing number of trendy pubs and music venues. It's undergone a lot of regeneration. The Biscuit Factory art gallery is close by on Stoddart Street in Shieldfield. This is also where the route slips over the edge of the Tyne Gorge. Use the Byker Link cycleway to descend onto the Quayside, where you head west under the famous Tyne bridges.

This is Newcastle in full splendour. To the world the Tyne Gorge and its bridges – the High Level, the Swing Bridge and the Tyne Bridge – are Newcastle. Their glory days were when this Quayside was a hive of industry, but now it's a place of leisure they have kept their looks.

Newcastle – locals don't feel the need to add the 'upon Tyne' – grew prosperous on coal, then on shipbuilding. The coal connection came from a deal done by the city elders back in the 1600s, whereby all coal mined in the north-east, if it was to be transported anywhere by sea, had to be loaded from this quay. Shipbuilding came later, and it was shared with Gateshead on the south

SECRET VALLEY AND SPLENDID QUAY

Track Elevation

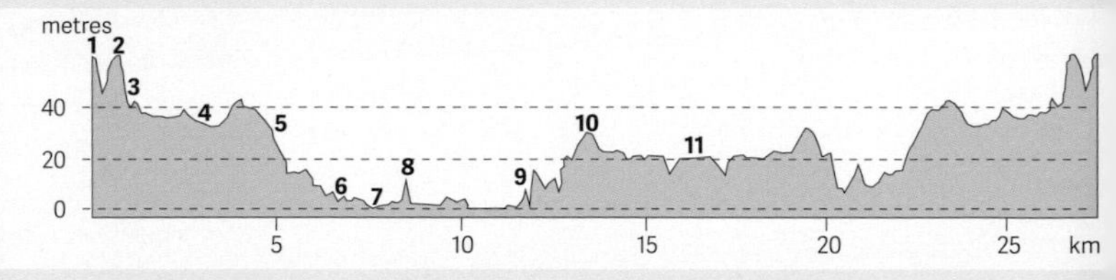

1 Start/Finish in South Gosforth

2 Follow street signs to Jesmond

3 Enter Jesmond Dene, head south

4 Armstrong and Heaton Parks

5 Street section to Byker link

6 Descend and turn right for Quayside

7 Millennium Bridge

8 Turn round after riding under the three old bridges

9 Continue straight

10 Follow Hadrian's Wall cycleway to Roman fort

11 Roman fort, turn around and retrace the route to South Gosforth

bank of the Tyne, and with Sunderland on the River Wear.

Those industries, and others that grew on the money they created, are mostly gone. For a while the Quayside was virtually derelict; then the rejuvenation of Newcastle began. The Co-operative Society building is now a sumptuous hotel – just one example of classic architecture in the city to have been repurposed – with the new buildings fitting in perfectly.

The Tyne also has a new bridge, the Gateshead Millennium, or the 'Blinking Eye', because that's what it looks like when the bridge tilts to let ships pass underneath. It's a glorious piece of civil engineering, created for pedestrians and cyclists to cross between Newcastle and Gateshead. The cycle path is particularly exhilarating, because when you ride over the water above a certain speed you cannot see the bridge: you only see water below you. It feels as though you're flying.

The Quayside is a delight to ride along, and passing under the three old bridges is special. It's also an experience to see fine buildings like the Baltic Flour Mill, which is now a centre for contemporary art. Just to the west, and on the same south side of the river, is Norman Foster's Sage-Gateshead Music Centre. The old buildings on the Newcastle side, meanwhile – the Cooperage and the old pubs – have been perfectly but

practically preserved, so they are fully used. There's a lot to take in, including various works of art dotted along the Quayside.

Once under the old bridges, turn round and retrace the route, passing the point where you came onto the Quayside, and head east. This is a section of a cross-country cycle-route that starts in Ravenglass in Cumbria on the north-west coast, and goes east to Tynemouth on the north-east.

The route follows Hadrian's Wall for much of its length, to Wallsend, just east of Newcastle, where the Wall ended with a Roman fort. Ride east to the fort, where the memories of Tyneside shipbuilding linger in Walker and Wallsend, and across the water in Jarrow. Then retrace to the Byker Link and north along Jesmond Dene, eventually arriving back at the starting-point in Gosforth.

44 The Bloody Bush Road

A long, mostly off-road ride from England into Scotland and back

DIFFICULTY RATING **9/10** WILDNESS RATING **8/10**

This is a big ride. Cycling from one country into another and back again on an historic trail is special. The Bloody Bush Road gives you that, plus a choice of starts on the Scottish or the English side. I chose the English start in Kielder Forest Park, which has many other wild-cycling opportunities, including a network of mountain-bike trails of varying difficulty.

Kielder is a long way from major population centres, which gives the place a really wild feel, and with no light pollution here it gets very dark at night. That led to the building of Kielder Observatory on Black Fell. It's well worth visiting while you are here.

The Bloody Bush ride is quite straightforward. It's suitable for cyclo-cross, gravel or mountain bikes, and the English start is in a car park where Lewis Burn flows into Kielder Water. Follow the trail up the left bank of Lewis Burn, going right at The Forks to cross Akenshaw Burn and continue up its valley. Keep right at the next trail fork, and on up the Bloody Bush Road. A lot of forest has been cleared, so the views are fantastic.

Eventually you reach the Bloody Bush Toll, where a huge pillar indicates the border with Scotland. A plaque on its northern side lists the old toll fees for crossing the border. And the name Bloody Bush itself refers to a gory incident that occurred during the days of the Border Reivers. See the next ride, number 45, for a full explanation of who the Border Reivers were.

A band of Northumbrian Reivers had been on a cattle raid in Liddesdale in Scotland, and were found sleeping here in the bushes by the men they had just robbed. The Scots slaughtered the Northumbrian Reivers and took back their cattle. Later, Bloody Bush

FACT FILE

Where Kielder is 20 miles north-west of Newcastle upon Tyne

OS grid ref NY 6469 9021

Start/Finish Lewis Burn car park

Ride distance 36.4 kilometres (22.74 miles)

Highest point Larriston Fells (460 metres)

Approximate time 4–5 hours

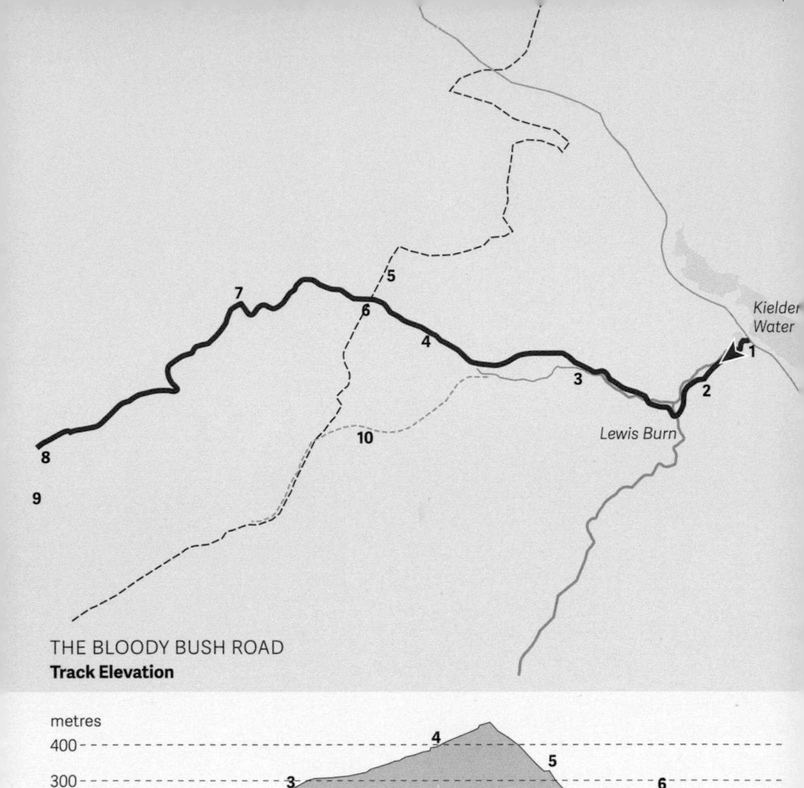

THE BLOODY BUSH ROAD

Track Elevation

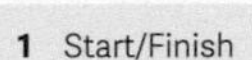

1 Start/Finish
2 Lewis Burn
3 Akenshaw Burn
4 Bloody Bush Road
5 Scotland/England border
6 Bloody Bush Toll
7 Sharp left off main forestry road
8 Dykecrofts turnaround
9 7 Stanes red trail to Kershope
10 Cross-Border Trail

Kielder is a long way from major population centres, which gives the place a really wild feel, and with no light pollution here it gets very dark at night.

Road was used to carry coal from Tynedale to fuel the woollen mills of the Scottish Borders.

The road continues to drag up after the toll, crossing the Larriston Fells, where you get a good feel for the Scottish Borders landscape, then plunges down. Finding your way down the long descent is relatively easy, so long as you don't miss the sharp left off the main forestry road that descends to Dinlabyre.

There are a couple of undulations after that; then you reach the turnaround point at the Dykecrofts visitor centre's car park. Retrace your outward journey back to Kielder. Because the nature of this trail suits a mountain bike best, mountain bikers could extend this ride by following the Newcastleton 7stanes red trail (see http://www.7stanes.com/) before crossing back to Kielder by the Cross-Border Trail.

Newcastleton is the base for one of Scotland's 7stanes mountain-bike trail centres. Follow the red trail, which goes south to a large, round stone. Go left at the stone and follow another trail going up the valley of Kershope Burn back into England, and down the Cross-Border Trail, and eventually to the car park you started in.

45 Border Reiver

A wild road ride worth experiencing for its own sake, or to access some incredible off-road trails

DIFFICULTY RATING **7/10** WILDNESS RATING **8/10**

This ride in sparsely populated Northumberland follows the River Coquet while delving into the early history of the Anglo-Scottish border lands. It's named after the families who divided this place into fiefdoms during the Middle Ages, who were called the Border Reivers.

With England and Scotland frequently at war, the livelihoods of people here were constantly disrupted, and in many cases destroyed, with no redress. This forced small communities, more or less family units, to look after their own interests, because their distant English king wouldn't. And they did so by cattle rustling.

FACT FILE

Where Upper Coquetdale in the Cheviot Hills, 40 kilometres north-west of Newcastle upon Tyne

OS grid ref NT 9194 0633

Start/Finish Car park, Alwinton

Ride distance 40 kilometres (25 miles)

Highest point Chew Green Roman fort (441 metres)

Approximate time 3–4 hours

'Reive' is an early-English word for robbery; 'ruffian' comes from the same source. Reiver Laws were written down, and the keystone of their legal system held that once a family had been robbed of their cattle they had six days to mount a counter-raid, if they could. If they couldn't, then ownership of the cattle passed to the raiders.

The counter-raid was called a Hot Trod, and it was done on horseback using sleuth hounds, called *slew dogge* in the Reiver dialect. The hounds were for tracking, because raiders didn't take stolen sheep or cattle straight to their settlements: they hid them in secret places until six days had passed. Looking at the ancient folded landscape today it's easy to see how the biggest herd could be made to disappear.

Reivers lived on both sides of the English–Scottish border, which Reiver Law said could be crossed with impunity to raid and counter-raid. By constantly warring with each other, albeit in accordance with agreed rules, the Reivers became great soldiers. The fiercest families fought for Scotland

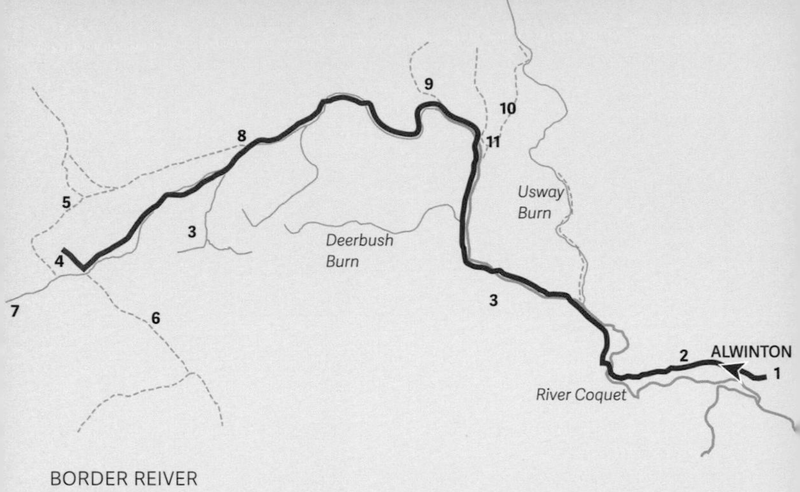

BORDER REIVER
Track Elevation

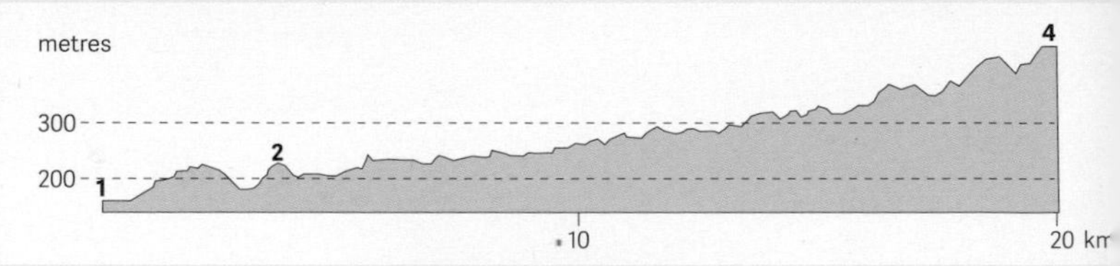

1 Start/Finish
2 First climb
3 Otterburn Ranges
3 Otterburn Ranges
4 Roman fort
5 Dere Street trail north
6 Dere Street trail south
7 Source of Coquet
8 Border Country Ride off-road loop re-joins road at Blindburn
9 Numerous bridleways into hills north of Coquet road
10 Border County Ride off-road trail
11 Barrowburn café down a farm track

or England as mercenaries, and they owed no allegiance, so would fight for whichever side paid most.

In return, the officials of both Scotland and England didn't bother the Reivers much. They became independent to the extent that Elizabeth I considered rebuilding Hadrian's Wall, which is south of Reiver country, and not even trying to police it.

But when James I of England (James VI of Scotland) took over the English throne, the Reivers overdid it. While the new king was still settling in, they saw a chance to expand, and went on a spree of rustling and land-grab. It was too much: King James went in hard against them, defeated the Reivers, and abolished their law. They were tamed, but their spirit seems to live here still.

That was a long history lesson, but the Reivers and this landscape fascinate me. It has changed little since Reiver times, so it's easy to imagine raid and counter-raid across this empty landscape; ruthless men travelling light on tough little ponies, their baying hounds leaping ahead, hungry for the scent. It must have been a fearsome sight.

Sorry, enough history now, but while I'm apologising, I'll mention the hills. You start in Alwinton. Head west on the only road out of the village, and there's a stiff climb after a kilometre, then a procession of them for the next 19. The return journey is easier.

The fiercest families fought for Scotland or England as mercenaries, and they owed no allegiance, so would fight for whichever side paid most.

The reward for the hills is worth it: setting aside my Reiver obsession, this road is special. It goes through Upper Coquetdale, following the river upstream, and where it ends, bridleways take over. Hardly anyone lives along it. When I did this ride, on 40 kilometres of metalled road I saw one tractor, two Land Rovers and three parked cars, plus a lost rep in a Volvo. I should add, though, that there was also one man driving a van who seemed possessed by the ghost of Ayrton Senna. He was going too fast, but at least I heard him coming, so could avoid him.

Bear that in mind should you hear a roaring engine's approach. The driver may have taken it for granted that nobody would be in his way; it's that quiet up here. There's no other road for miles around, so no human noise. Nothing except sheep and birds. When you can't hear any evidence of people at all, that's wild.

Upper Coquetdale is sheep country: white-faced Cheviots and Scottish blackfaces have grazed here since the 13th century. You'll see several circular stone pens called stells, where sheep shelter from the worst blizzards. This

This is a vast tract of military land used for blank ammunition and pyrotechnic practice. If you see a red flag flying, don't use any off-road trails on that side.

area is also known as the White Lands, not just because of snow in winter, but because the grass high up bleaches pale yellow during autumn, and by winter it's almost white.

The south side of the Coquet road borders Otterburn Ranges. This is a vast tract of military land used for blank ammunition and pyrotechnic practice. If you see a red flag flying, don't use any off-road trails on that side. Otherwise you can use the tracks across the ranges.

Road and river intertwine as they weave up the valley towards the Coquet's source, which is close to Chew Green, where the Romans built a fort on a road they called Dere Street. The road connected York with the Antonine Wall, which was built across the central belt of Scotland, and for a while represented the northern extent of the Roman Empire.

You can explore Dere Street north and south of the fort, as bridleways

stretch from it across the high, undulating landscape. Coquet Head, the source of the river, can be visited using another bridleway going west.

Another good off-road adventure can be had by following Dere Street north, then north-west, then north, where it follows the Scottish border. Go sharp right where two trails join, and follow this new track down to the Coquet Road at Blindburn. There are other off-road loops further down the road: the OS map shows them all. The Border Country Ride is an absolute joy to follow in good weather, but it's tough and technical in places. You have to know what you are doing.

Retracing from Chew Green, there's a lovely café in Barrowburn if you fancy a stop; otherwise continue down the way you came from Alwinton. The former village vicarage there is built on the site of a Bastle House, one of the small impregnable homes that the Reivers built. Cattle lived on the ground floor, and the people lived above. No stairs: just an outside ladder they pulled up after them. And no windows: just slits to fire arrows from. Proud and impregnable thievers: ladies and gentlemen, I give you – the Border Reivers!

10

Scotland

46 Edinburgh by Innertube

One leg of an extensive network of cycle paths running through Edinburgh's bustle and wilder places

DIFFICULTY RATING **3/10** WILDNESS RATING **4/10**

Edinburgh is a wonderful city to explore, but in particular it's wonderful to explore by bike nowadays, because of a visionary 70-kilometre network of cycleways called the Innertube. It's so easy to use because of its London Underground-inspired map. It shows each route with a separate colour, all the junctions and access points, and even denotes stretches that are still under construction.

The Innertube is made up of converted railway lines and park paths, so as well as providing infrastructure for a green transport system, which also lowers congestion on the city's roads, it provides bike access to Edinburgh's wilder places. It was thought up and created by the recycling charity Bike Station, and it's just brilliant.

There's a map of the whole Edinburgh Innertube on www.innertubemap.com, showing how some routes radiate from the city centre, while others do the same from outlying areas, and how they interact with one another as well as other cycle routes. It's possible to use the Innertube for real adventures, by riding from the city centre out into the countryside and returning by another Innertube route.

I've chosen one leg of the Innertube for this book, a ride from the city centre to the seaside, because who doesn't like going to the seaside? Most of the ride uses the Haymarket-to-Crammond route, and it's very easy to follow.

I started from Balbirnie Place and just followed the signs. The Old Town with its ancient buildings and monuments is a couple of kilometres due east, and behind that stands the mass of Arthur's Seat and Holyrood Park. Together they are the landmarks

FACT FILE

Where Edinburgh is the capital of Scotland

OS grid ref NT 2313 7335

Start/Finish Balbirnie Place Innertube access point

Ride distance 14.25 kilometres (8 miles)

Highest point Middle of Roseburn Path (62 metres)

Approximate time 1.5–2 hours

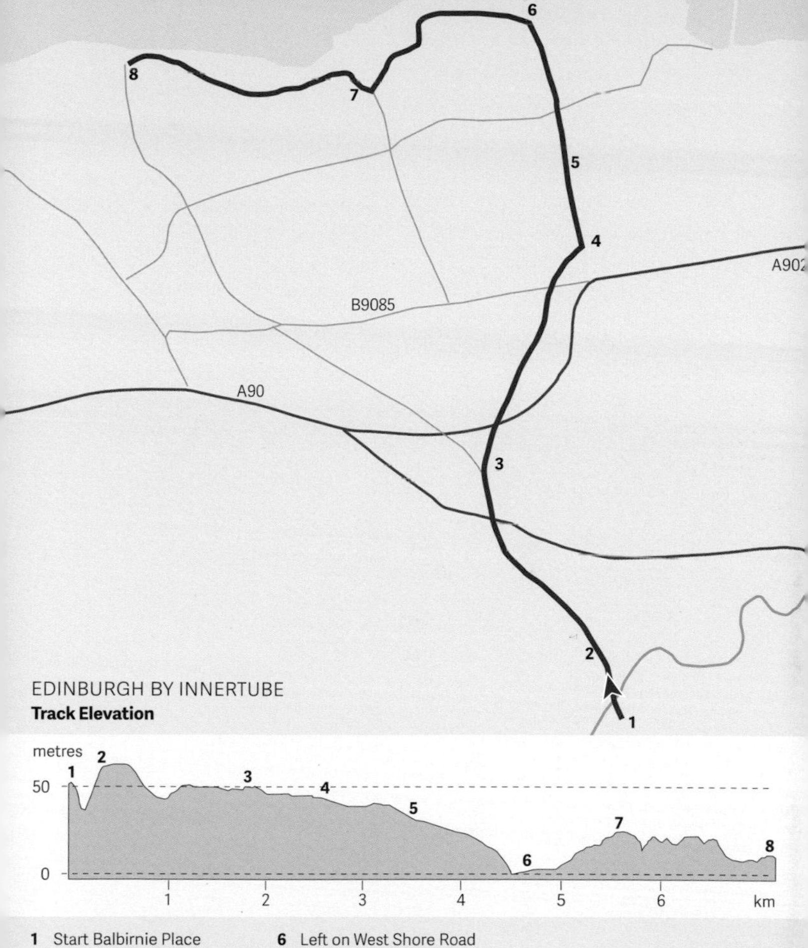

1 Start Balbirnie Place
2 Roseburn Path
3 Take the right fork, the left goes to the Forth Bridges
4 Turn left, right goes to Leith
5 Complicated section but well signed
6 Left on West Shore Road
7 Right on Marine Drive
8 Retrace or go south to Cramond and another trail to Forth Bridges

I've chosen one leg of the Innertube for this book, a ride from the city centre to the seaside, because who doesn't like going to the seaside?

of Edinburgh, and it's possible to explore Holyrood Park using the Holyrood-to-Musselburgh leg of the Innertube. For this route, though, head north-west along the tree-lined Roseburn Path, then take the right fork after the Craigleith junction access point. Another Innertube cycle path goes left all the way to the Forth Bridges.

Go left at the next fork, because the right leads to the Port of Leith, then head north – your nose will lead you towards the salty tang of the Forth estuary. Turn left when you get there to ride along West Shore Road, then right onto Marine Drive, and continue to the terminus of this ride at a roundabout. Retrace, or go left to pick up the Innertube cycle path to Crammond and the Forth Bridges. The cycle path leads to the road bridge, and crossing the Forth by bike is unforgettable.

47 Fruid, Talla and the Jubilee Road

Experience the tranquillity of the upper Tweed Valley in a very special place

DIFFICULTY RATING **7/10** WILDNESS RATING **6/10**

Consider this ride a hub for other adventures. The Moffat Hills – all of the Scottish Borders, in fact – are full of incredible out-of-the-way places to ride. I've located the hub here because I've rarely experienced a place as tranquil as Talla Reservoir. When I first saw it from above on Fans Law, it took my breath away, and riding alongside Talla is pure medicine for the mind.

I've started the ride from the A701 Tweed Valley road, because there are parking possibilities in lay-bys there. Otherwise you can park at Megget Reservoir above the Talla valley and ride down to join it. Failing that, the towns of Moffat and Peebles are fairly close by.

Cross the Tweed from Tweedsmuir, turn right straight after the bridge, then take the second left after almost 2 kilometres of riding. At this point you could extend the ride by carrying straight on to explore Fruid Reservoir, which is even more off the beaten track than Talla. A word about bikes for this one: if you stick to the metalled roads then any bike will do, but for the Jubilee Road section you need a cyclo-cross, gravel or mountain bike.

The right turn takes you onto the Jubilee Road, which traces an interesting course through a conifer plantation on the six hills between Fruid and Talla. The road, which is a forest track really, was built around the hills but it's still a 5-kilometre uphill slog, with some undulations to reach its summit.

The road then undulates for over 3 kilometres through a series of exciting descents into five hairpin bends with steep climbs out of each one, before

FACT FILE

Where Tweedsmuir is 14 miles south-west of Peebles and 10 miles north-east of Moffat, which is junction 15 of the A74(M)

OS grid ref NT 0968 2432

Start/Finish Tweedsmuir bridge over the River Tweed

Ride distance 32 kilometres (20 miles)

Highest points Laird's Creuch Rig (505 metres). Much of this ride is above 400 metres

Approximate time 3–4 hours

FRUID, TALLA AND THE JUBILEE ROAD

Track Elevation

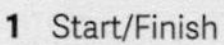

1 Start/Finish
2 Bridge across the Tweed
3 Go straight on for the outward leg
4 Long steep uphill
5 End of long uphill, beginning of undulation
6 Garelet Hill
7 Start of downhill
8 Start of very steep downhill
9 Turnaround unless you want to go further
10 Talla Reservoir road
11 Top of steep Talla Water climb

A word about bikes for this one: if you stick to the metalled roads then any bike will do, but for the Jubilee Road section you need a cyclo-cross, gravel or mountain bike.

---

some consistent downhill. The first 3 kilometres of the descent aren't so steep, but the last two are. So take care.

Close to the bottom there's a very sharp right next to Menzion Burn, and you follow the course of the burn down to Menzion and turn right. Go right again just before the bridge over the Tweed you came in on, and follow this road uphill to cross the Talla Reservoir dam. Now you'll see and feel the tranquillity of Talla. It's incredible.

Ride along this road until you've soaked up enough to recall in times of stress, and turn around and head back to Tweedsmuir. Or, if you are feeling strong, carry on and climb up the Talla Water road. It's incredibly steep, over 20% in the middle, and the climb is 750 metres long, but stop at the top on the tiny bridge across Talla Water, and look back. What you see will take away what little breath you have left.

48 Loch Katrine by Boat and Bike

Take the ferry across Loch Katrine and ride back around its banks

DIFFICULTY RATING **6/10** WILDNESS RATING **8/10**

Any cycling that starts with a ferry crossing is wild in my book. This is worth doing in its own right, and it's a terrific introduction to wild cycling, because you can hire a bike where the ferry departs. Then it's not difficult to ride back on the cycleway from Stronachlachar to Trossachs Pier, so this one is suitable for a whole range of abilities. Additionally, like other rides in the more mountainous districts in this book, it's an introduction to the wild-cycling opportunities around it.

I discovered Loch Katrine during a ride over Duke's Pass from Aberfoyle, when I diverted to ride the Loch Katrine cycleway from Trossachs Pier to Stronachlachar and back. Then I continued east along the length of Loch Venacher, around the back of Callander and back to Aberfoyle.

Aberfoyle, Duke's Pass, Loch Venacher, Callander, the Lake of Menteith, then back to Aberfoyle, is the route taken by Scotland's oldest time trial race, the Tour of the Trossachs. In keeping with this bit of cycling history, the Loch Lomond and Trossachs National Park is very bike-friendly, with a number of carefully thought-out routes for all abilities. Check them out on www.lochlomond-trossachs.org.

For now, though, it's all aboard *Lady of the Lake*, named after the 1810 poem inspired by the serene majesty of Loch Katrine, or another boat, *Sir Walter Scott*, named after the man who wrote the poem. Sailing times and all other information you need to plan this ride are on www.lochkatrine.com.

There's a car park at the eastern edge of Loch Katrine, and others close by. Enjoy the wonderful outward journey to Stronachlachar Pier, where

FACT FILE

Where Loch Katrine is 10 kilometres north of Aberfoyle, which is about 50 kilometres north of the outskirts of Glasgow

OS grid ref NN 4955 0716

Start/Finish Trossachs Pier

Ride distance 32 kilometres (20 miles)

Highest point Almost exactly halfway back to Trossachs Pier (210 metres)

Approximate time 2–3 hours, plus the ferry crossing

there's a café if you need a bit of fortification before the ride. Then head north on the cycleway, which has a good surface for most of its length.

If you've time before setting off, it's worth riding west from Stronachlachar Pier to Inversnaid at the north end of Loch Lomond, using the Old Military Road, one of many that cross Scotland. It adds an extra 16 kilometres there and back to this ride, but lovely Loch Arklet and the sudden view of the 1,000-metre peak of Ben Ime on the other side of Loch Lomond are spectacular.

Back on this ride you go round the head of Loch Katrine, where Glen Gyle Water enters it, and as you start down the other side of Loch Katrine more of the deep valley around it, Strath Gartney, is revealed.

Continuing south-east, the trail starts climbing through some woodland to a high point of 210 metres. At this point you are 340 metres, so 1,115 feet, above the bed of Loch Katrine. The loch is 13 kilometres long and 1 kilometre across at its widest point. It used to be famous for cattle thievery – Katrine comes from the Gaelic word for cattle thief – and for Rob Roy McGregor, who was born in Glengyle House at the head of it.

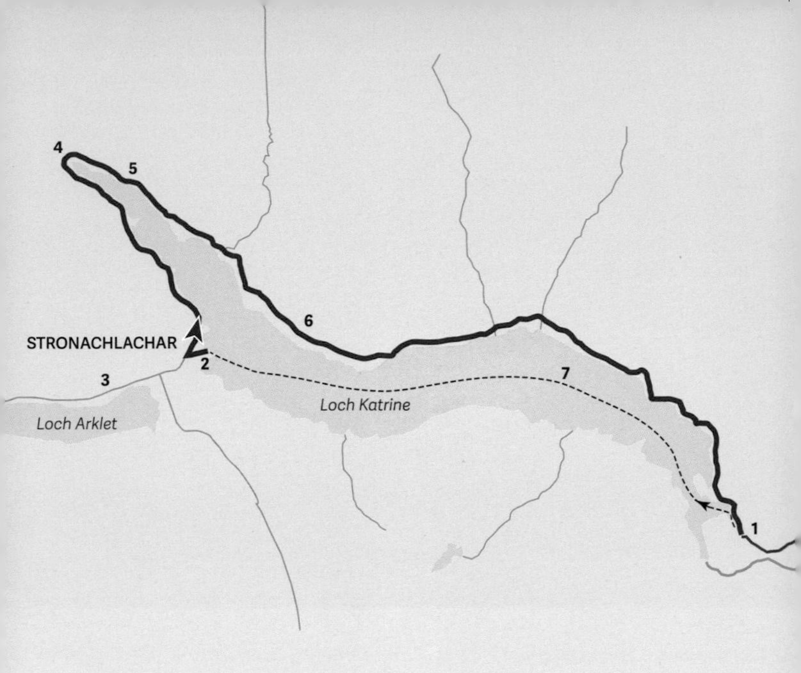

LOCH KATRINE
Track Elevation

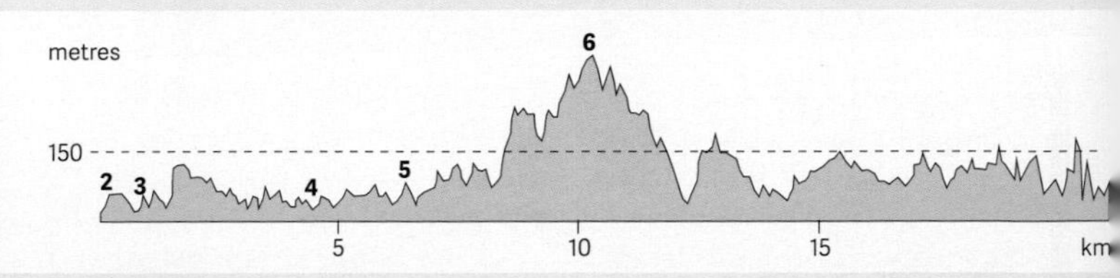

1 Start/Finish
2 Ferry landing and start of ride
3 Military road
4 Head of loch
5 Birthplace of Rob Roy McGregor
6 Highest point of ride
7 Deepest part of Loch Katrine

McGregor was dashing but unfortunate in life. He borrowed money from the Duke of Montrose to expand his cattle herd, but the man trusted to buy the cattle disappeared with the cash. The Duke's men threw McGregor off his land, and he feuded with the Duke until he was imprisoned in 1722.

Rob Roy, as he became known, has since been turned into a Scottish Robin Hood by the fictionalised accounts of his life, notably by Sir Walter Scott. There have been three *Rob Roy* films; the most recent, in 1995, had Liam Neeson in the starring role. The Rob Roy cocktail, meanwhile, was invented by a Waldorf Hotel bartender in 1894 to celebrate the opening in New York of the Rob Roy Operetta.

The loch is even deeper further west, 140 metres near Brenachoile Lodge, where the trail surface becomes slightly rougher. It's still very rideable and enjoyable, though, as it passes through a wide belt of mixed woodland. Look out for red squirrels; it's a perfect habitat for them. There's plenty of food, plus shelter from the ospreys, which you might see on the more open sections of this ride.

The final section of the cycleway hugs the loch shore, although it still undulates a fair bit. If you've time after returning to Trossachs Pier there's a wonderful ride around Loch Venacher. Or further south, try the Queen Elizabeth Forest Park. Then there's the challenging Glen Finglas route, which is mountain-bike territory and not for the faint-hearted, or faint-legged.

The Glen Finglas route starts in Brig o' Turk, which is only 5 kilometres from the end of this ride along the A821. It's worth a visit just to see the Bike Tree, growing in what was the village blacksmith's garden. The story goes that a man leant his bike against this tree before going off to fight in the First World War, and never came back to collect it. The tree grew around the bike, and now the bike and the tree are one.

49 Remembering Jason

A road ride – all roads in this part of Scotland are wild, with spectacular views

DIFFICULTY RATING **7/10** WILDNESS RATING **7/10**

I first saw this part of Scotland in 2007 when writing a story about Jason McIntyre for *Cycling Weekly* magazine. Jason was an incredibly talented cyclist who, independent of the British Cycling system that has produced so many world and Olympic champions, beat the best in Britain to win two British time-trial championships in 2006 and 2007.

Jason was outside the British Cycling system because he chose to live away from its Manchester base in Fort William so he could help care for his daughter who was very ill. It was a tragedy when Jason was killed in a road accident while training near his home in January 2008.

You meet some remarkable people in life, and Jason McIntyre stands out in mine. He loved his family, his sport and his life, and he loved training on the roads of Ardgour Sunart and Moidart. Jason's favourite ride was a wild jaunt around the edges of those places, mountains on one side of him, the sea on the other, but his ride is over 80 miles long and there's no way of cutting it short, so I've chosen a version of Jason's ride on the other side of Loch Sunart. At 61 kilometres it's still the longest in this book, and it starts at the same place as Jason's did: the jetty in Corran. That's where the Corran ferry docks after the short crossing of Loch Linnhe, and the crossing is an incredible way to start this ride, with the mountains of Ben Nevis behind you.

Route-finding is easy. Head left on the A861 to ride alongside Loch Linnhe, then follow this road inland along Glen Tarbet. I bet it's the quietest A-road you'll ever ride on in Britain, apart from the next one. At 20 kilometres turn left on the A884, just

FACT FILE

Where Corran Ferry crossing, 21 kilometres (13 miles) south-west of Fort William on the A82

OS grid ref NN 0606 6365

Start/Finish Corran Jetty

Ride distance 32 kilometres (20 miles)

Highest point A884 pass (272 metres)

Approximate time 3–4 hours (not counting the ferry)

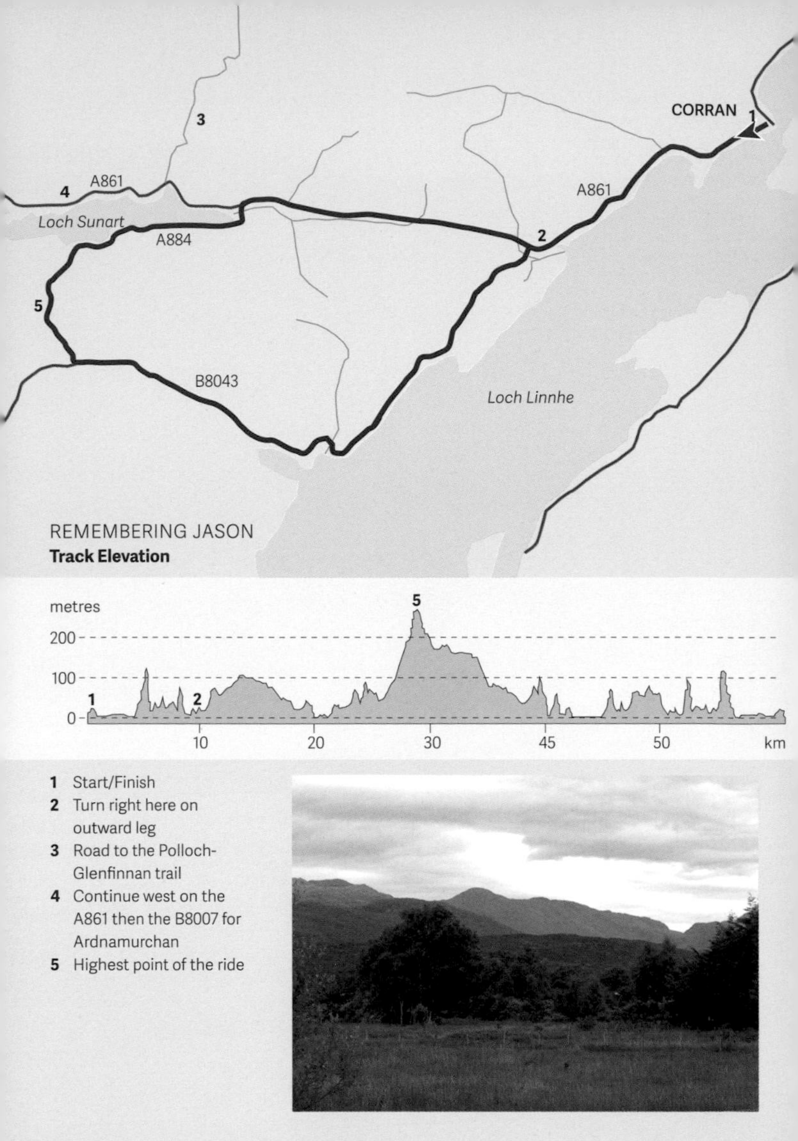

CORRAN
1
3
4
A861
Loch Sunart
A884
A861
2
5
B8043
Loch Linnhe
REMEMBERING JASON
Track Elevation
metres
5
200
100
0
1
2
10
20
30
45
50
km
1 Start/Finish
2 Turn right here on outward leg
3 Road to the Polloch-Glenfinnan trail
4 Continue west on the A861 then the B8007 for Ardnamurchan
5 Highest point of the ride

short of Strontian. Jason's ride carried on west towards the Ardnamurchan Peninsula, the furthest west you can go in mainland Britain, and a terrific wild-cycling destination itself. Or, if you turn right in Strontian and follow a crazy, twisting road through Polloch to Loch Shiel, there's a right-of-way trail going north to Glenfinnan at the head of the loch.

The wild-cycling possibilities here are huge but, continuing with this example, carry on along Loch Sunart, then head inland just before Liddesdale to start its only really serious climb, which crosses the pass between Beinn nam Beathrach and Taobh Dubh. Turn left 2 kilometres after the summit and descend to Kingairloch on the Loch a' Choire inlet, then continue along Loch Linnhe north-east back to Corran and the ferry. The last crossing is at 9.20 p.m.; details on www.locharbertransport.org.uk.

... the Corran ferry docks after the short crossing of Loch Linnhe, and the crossing is an incredible way to start this ride, with the mountains of Ben Nevis behind you.

50 Cape Wrath

The epitome of wild cycling and the only place where we could end

DIFFICULTY RATING **8/10** WILDNESS RATING **10/10**

Cape Wrath is the north-west tip of mainland UK. One of only two capes in the entire country, it's a majestic place where a rock-armoured arrow-head of tall cliffs stands guard against the North Sea's eternal fight with the Atlantic Ocean.

The country behind Cape Wrath is as near to true wilderness as any place in Britain. The empty landscape is called the Parph. There may be military activity on some days, but otherwise nobody lives in the entire 107 square miles of this ancient and other-worldly landscape. Cape Wrath has always been a magnet for adventurous cyclists, and in 1949 it inspired the foundation of a fellowship dedicated to the experience of cycling along Britain's wildest road. Created by Rex Coley, the Cape Wrath Fellowship still exists today.

Rex Coley wrote for a magazine called *Cycling* under the pseudonym Ragged Staff, which was taken from the bear-and-ragged-staff coat of arms of his native Warwickshire. Coley loved cycle touring, which is what he wrote about in books like *Cycling is Such Fun* (1947), or *Joyous Cycling* (1953). The latter has a foreword by Reg Harris, a six-times world sprint champion on the track, but an avid touring cyclist before his racing career really took off, and again after its end.

As you might gather from his book titles, Coley's greatest desire was to promote the joy of cycling. As racing increasingly became a serious sport, so, he felt, the club runs and cycle touring he enjoyed were featuring less in British cycling life. He wasn't alone: in 1955 the Rough Stuff Fellowship – along with Coley a patron spirit of wild cycling in the UK – was founded. Its

FACT FILE

Where The far north-west of Scotland. The nearest town of any size is Lairg, and that's well over 60 miles south-east of Cape Wrath

OS grid ref NC 3778 6618

Start/Finish Keoldale

Ride distance 36 kilometres (22.5 miles) there and back

Highest points 174 metres (8.76 kilometres into the ride)

Approximate time 4–6 hours

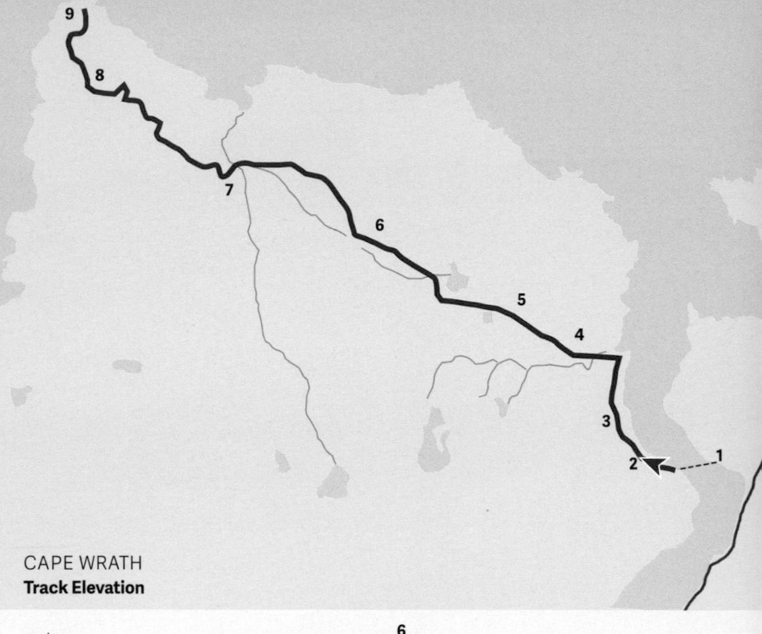

CAPE WRATH
Track Elevation

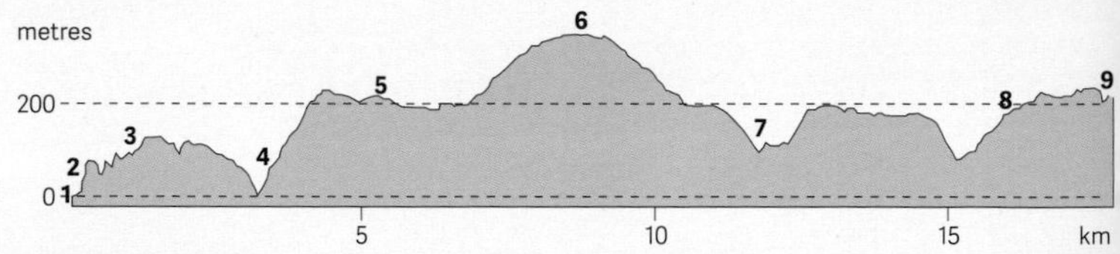

1 Start/Finish
2 Very steep climb
3 Exposed cross winds
4 Second steep climb
5 Flatter section
6 Highest point of the ride
7 Very steep at bottom of this descent
8 Final climb
9 Turnaround

objective was to preserve the spirit of using bikes for adventure, and not just as tools for racing.

Doing this ride is all you need to join the Cape Wrath Fellowship. It's straightforward but not easy. The weather is capricious, to say the least. The road is very narrow, and very rough in places, with plenty of puncture-causing sharp stones. You can use almost any bike for this ride, but it must have heavy-duty tyres that are in good condition. There are hills, though, and sometimes strong winds. All in all it's a tough proposition.

The first difficulty is getting onto the same piece of land as the road. That involves crossing the Kyle of Durness on the Keoldale ferry, which operates from May to September. It's a motor boat now, but was a rowing boat in Coley's day. See capewrathferry.wordpress.com for the sailing times. Remember to time your journey there and back between sailings.

The ferry crosses to a jetty, where the road to Cape Wrath begins. Built in 1828 to service Cape Wrath lighthouse, it is 18 kilometres (11.25 miles) long. Stone causeways are used to cross boggy land, and man-made embankments help with the steepest gradients, although there are still some fearsome hills.

One of the toughest comes straight off the ferry, and climbs at an average of 11% for over 300 metres, with sections of over 20%. The road drags up a bit further, then follows the cliff tops before plunging down to cross the

Daill River. This is followed by another climb of just over a kilometre with an average gradient of 10.5%. That's two back-breaking climbs and only 4.3 kilometres completed …

The next section of road crosses some flat boggy ground, before a 2.5-kilometre climb between two hills, Maovalley and Sgribhis-bheinn. They both have the distinctive rounded shape of hills in this area, which is the oldest landscape in Europe. The underlying rock here, Lewisian gneiss, is over 3 billion years old.

The top of the climb is the highest point of this ride, but the hills are by no means over. A long descent, which gets very steep close to the bottom, leads to a bridge over the Kearvig River. Then there's another steep climb before plunging down the last stream crossing, followed by the final pull to a promontory above Cape Wrath lighthouse.

To gain membership of the Cape Wrath Fellowship a photograph at the lighthouse had to be sent to Rex Coley at *Cycling* magazine, and he awarded a certificate and a badge. Responsibility for the Fellowship passed to another *Cycling* journalist, Peter Knottley, after Coley died in 1985, but it lapsed when Knottley retired in 1992. Thankfully, it was revived two years later by the Cyclists' Touring Club, now Cycling UK, which runs the Fellowship today.